RADICAL EQUALITY IN EDUCATION

"Joanne Larson's *Radical Equality in Education* presents a timely and truly paradigm-changing approach to education. It is a must read for all those who realize schools should not exist to produce service workers but to produce proactive citizens capable of transforming the world they live in."

James Paul Gee, Mary Lou Fulton Presidential Professor of
Literacy Studies, Arizona State University, USA

"Brave, timely, innovative and important. This book is a necessary statement that helps point us where we need to be heading in education, and argued by an author superbly placed to make the case. It will contribute to a debate that needs to occur, and occur now."

Colin Lankshear, James Cook University, Australia

Tinkering with the current educational system from within has not provided a just and equitable education for all children. In this book, acclaimed education theorist Joanne Larson poses basic questions about the nature and purpose of schooling. Proposing that what is needed is a new purpose that is more consistent with contemporary knowledge production processes—one that moves beyond the either/or binary of preparing workers/citizens in a competitive global economy or a democracy, Larson argues that the only real solution is to start over in U.S. education—the purpose of schooling should be to facilitate human learning, meaning making, and knowledge production toward just and equitable education for all.

Radical Equality in Education offers a new ontological starting point and a new theoretical framing that would follow from it, articulates theoretical, curricular, pedagogical, and assessment principles that frame a real plan for fundamental change in American education, and presents examples of what these ideas might look like in schools and communities.

Joanne Larson is Michael W. Scandling Professor of Education, University of Rochester, Warner Graduate School of Education and Human Development, USA.

RADICAL EQUALITY IN EDUCATION

Starting Over in U.S. Schooling

Joanne Larson

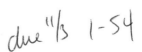

 Routledge
Taylor & Francis Group

NEW YORK AND LONDON

First published 2014
by Routledge
711 Third Avenue, New York, NY 10017

and by Routledge
2 Park Square, Milton Park, Abingdon, Oxon OX14 4RN

Routledge is an imprint of the Taylor & Francis Group, an informa business

© 2014 Taylor & Francis

The right of Joanne Larson to be identified as author of this work has
been asserted by her in accordance with sections 77 and 78 of the
Copyright, Designs and Patents Act 1988.

Library of Congress Cataloging-in-Publication Data
Larson, Joanne, 1956–
Radical equality in education : starting over in U.S. schooling /
 Joanne Larson.
    pages cm
  Includes bibliographical references and index.
  1. Educational equalization—United States. 2. Educational change—
United States. 3. Critical pedagogy—United States. I. Title.
   LC213.2.L38 2014
   379.2′6—dc23
   2013033713

ISBN: 978-0-415-52803-0 (hbk)
ISBN: 978-0-415-52804-7 (pbk)
ISBN: 978-0-203-11867-2 (ebk)

Typeset in Bembo
by Apex CoVantage, LLC

Printed and bound in the United States of America by Publishers Graphics,
LLC on sustainably sourced paper.

CONTENTS

Dedication

To the children and youth of the future

ILLUSTRATIONS

Tables

Figures

FOREWORD

Toward a Humanist and Consequential View of Learning and Equality

Kris Gutiérrez

Radical Equality in Education lays out an impassioned and thoughtful argument for a new pedagogical imagination organized around a democratic vision of schooling and society and a more humanist view of learning. It is both a moral plea for justice and a call to action for a more robust notion of educational equity. However, the argument advanced in this book is more than rethinking another wave of school reform, as Larson notes, the kind of formulaic "tinkering" that glosses over historical and current inequities and the structures and practices that sustain inequality. Instead, Larson calls for a reorganization of the functional system, a social systems reorganization in which schools take on a central role in advancing a comprehensive vision of social, economic, and intellectual equality.

The broad imbalance of power relations in this society has resulted in economic, spatial, and educational wastelands in which students, workers, and citizens in non-dominant communities are positioned as the objects of injustice with inequitable access to resources. The example of the urban "food desert" serves both as a salient case of new forms of community empowerment and as a metaphor for a new understanding of learning as the design of new social futures (Gutiérrez, 2008; O'Connor & Allen, 2010). Those of us taking a humanist approach to learning and development, particularly within the cultural historical activity theoretical approach, theorize consequential learning as the reorganization of everyday and scientific or formal knowledge (Gutiérrez, 2008, 2012). This view is central to Larson's approach in which she argues for relevance and situated views of learning. In some respects, her approach, which invokes Rancière (1991), resonates with Rogoff et al.'s (2003) notion of *community intent participation* in which people learn by participating in the routine practices of a community, pitching in through a variety of ways that are valued and extended over time. These forms of learning are highly relational and the expectation is that everyone can contribute and learn by being part of the practice. Unlike Rancière (at least this is underspecified in his work), the social organization of practice and the forms of assistance available are central to the changing nature of participation over time (Rogoff, 2003).

In contrast to traditional views of learning, particularly those instantiated in schools, learning necessarily involves the development of and a mutual relation between school-based (vertical) and everyday knowledge (horizontal) and expertise. In other words, transformative learning, as elaborated in this book, involves shifts between and across new combinations of contexts and tools that can be leveraged across spaces and places and domains of learning. Within this view, learning is respectful and part of the everyday.

A number of us have been theorizing a related and relevant concept of "Connected Learning" (Ito et al., 2013) to address the disconnect that youth experience as they move across ecologies and practices. We theorize "Connected Learning" as an approach to addressing inequity in education in ways geared to a networked society. It seeks to leverage the potential of digital media to expand access to learning that is socially embedded, interest-driven, and oriented toward educational, economic, or political opportunity (p. 1).

"Connected Learning" is particularly relevant to views of learning advanced in *Radical Equality,* as we need new ways of understanding the intercultural, hybrid, and multimodal practices in which youth participate. In my own work, I use the metaphor of "learning as movement" (Gutiérrez, 2008; Vossoughi & Gutiérrez, in press) to highlight that today's youth move across a range of contexts and produce artifacts that reflect the interests and repertoires of practice developed across nodes of interests and influence, including peer culture and academic domains of inquiry. Attending to this horizontal movement is key to empowering new forms of participation in academic as well as civic and social life.

Bringing spatiality into understandings of learning reflects an important new move in both learning theory and more equitable and humanist approaches to research. Drawing on Soja (2010), the importance of spatial justice as a right is exemplified in the account of a community–researcher partnership that coalesced around the development of the corner store, or the "cornerstone" as the members of the participating African American community reframed it. This reframing of the store as a space and place of political, sociocultural, and educational nourishment and sustenance indexes the ways people can become historical actors, producers, and designers of their own new futures—a central theme of this book.

The consequences of economic and spatial segregation are central to understanding persistent inequality in the United States. As Orfield and Lee (2005) have reported, the levels of educational segregation for African American and Latino students have been increasing since the 1980s; their work documents this growing inequality by linking standardized achievement scores and the racial composition of the school, as well as the availability of experienced and highly qualified teachers in the schools (p. 5). As they note, the nation's highest dropout rates are located in majority minority high schools in urban areas. Exacerbated by high levels of poverty and persistent housing segregation, students in these schools, according to Orfield and Lee, have limited access to a range of experiences, resources, practices, and opportunities that they can leverage to shape and reshape new trajectories.

In this highly segregated mass educational system, as Larson elaborates, schooling becomes encapsulated, to use Engeström's (1991) notion, in ways that make learning inert, inconsequential, and difficult to link to everyday practices. As Engeström (1991) argues, school acquired knowledge often "fails to become a living instrumentality for making sense of the . . . natural and social phenomena encountered by students outside school" (p. 250). From a cultural historical perspective, *Radical Equality* calls for expansive forms of learning that require the object of school learning to be "radically widened" in ways that reframe the purpose of schooling as "the facilitation of human learning, meaning making, and knowledge production toward just and equitable education for all students," to use Larson's terms.

Rupturing the encapsulation of school is theorized in Larson's work as instantiating a form of radical equality. Informed by French theorist Rancière's (1991) theories of radical equality, Larson calls for a new ontological and epistemological stance centered on more symmetrical understandings of knowledge production and equipotential and dynamic participation structures as the new foundation of a new U.S. educational system. This pedagogical vision challenges economic and assimilationist goals and reorients schooling toward understandings that meaning making and human learning are relevant and valuable educational goals.

Radical Equality in Education lays out a vision, both utopian and concrete—a vision where notions of intelligence are reframed and the social organization of everyday and civic life not only allows full participation but where valued and consequential learning is the norm.

References

Engeström, Y. (1991). Non scholae sed vitae discimus: Toward overcoming the encapsulation of school learning. *Learning and Instruction, 1,* 243–259.

Gutiérrez, K. (2008). Developing a sociocritical literacy in the third space. *Reading Research Quarterly, 43(2),* 148–164.

Gutiérrez, K. (2012). Leveraging horizontal and everyday practices: Toward a theory of connected learning. Paper presented at the annual meeting of the Literacy Research Association, San Diego, California, November 28, 2012.

Ito, M., Gutiérrez, K., Livingstone, S., Penuel, W., Rhodes, J, Salen, K., Schor, J., Sefton-Green, J., & Watkins, C. (2013). *Connected learning: An agenda for research and design.* Irvine, CA: The Digital Media and Learning Research Hub Reports on Connected Learning.

O'Connor, K. & Allen, A. (2010). Learning as the organizing of social futures. In W. Penuel & K. O'Connor (Eds.), *Yearbook of the National Society for the Study of Education,* 108 (pp. 160–175). New York: Teachers College Press.

Orfield, G. & Lee, C. (2005). *Why segregation matters: Poverty and educational inequality.* The Civil Rights Project. Cambridge, MA: Harvard University Press.

Rancière, J. (1991). *The ignorant schoolmaster: Five lessons in intellectual emancipation.* Stanford, CA: Stanford University Press.

Rogoff, B. (2003). *The cultural nature of human development.* New York: Oxford University Press.

Rogoff, B., Paradise, R., Mejía Arauz, R., Correa-Chávez, M., & Angelillo, C. (2003). Firsthand learning through intent participation. *Annual Review of Psychology, 54,* 175–203.

Soja, E. (2010). *Seeking spatial justice.* Minneapolis: University of Minnesota Press.

Vossoughi, S. & Gutiérrez, K. (in press). Toward a multi-sited ethnographic sensibility. In J. Vadeboncoeur (Ed.), *NSEE Yearbook.* New York: Teachers College Press.

PREFACE

The purpose of this book is threefold: (1) to make an argument for why we need to start over in U.S. education; (2) to offer a new ontological starting point and a new theoretical framing that would follow from this new ontological position; and (3) to present examples of what these ideas might look like in schools and communities. The book poses basic questions about the nature and purpose of schooling and articulates a plausible reconceptualization of U.S. public education. With the changed ontological and epistemological stances, I propose we need a new purpose of schooling that is more consistent with contemporary knowledge production processes, one that moves beyond the either/or binary of preparing workers/citizens in a competitive global economy or a democracy, respectively.

Chapter 1 lays out the argument for why we need to start over. I briefly describe the state of schools today and the detrimental consequences on children and youth of staying the current course. I offer three main arguments for starting over: (1) Schools are outdated and have not responded adequately to changes in society associated with advanced Internet communication technologies; (2) Schools do not equitably serve the interests of children and youth; and (3) The purpose of schooling to produce workers and/or citizens has not been achieved and is thus unproductive. Questions guiding this book include: (1) Who benefits from keeping schools the way they are (both economically and via social and cultural capital)? And (2) If the social contract between society and schools has been irrevocably broken, who is benefitting from keeping a broken system? By social contract I mean the mutual understanding that "we the people" trust that schools will educate our children and youth well and that schools will do no harm. Chapter 2 brings together concepts from the French theorist Rancière (1991) on radical equality with theories about knowledge production, equipotential participation, and mass collaboration to articulate a new ontological and epistemological stance that might ground a new U.S. educational system.

Drawing from the theoretical framework articulated in Chapter 2, I argue in Chapter 3 that the purpose of schooling should be *to facilitate human learning, meaning making, and knowledge production toward just and equitable education for all.* I place key emphasis here on social justice, as I believe the current U.S. education system functions to perpetuate injustice and, I argue, this must change. Furthermore, this purpose moves away from economic (worker) or assimilationist (citizen) motives toward the view that human learning, meaning making, and knowledge production are valuable in and of themselves as educational goals. Chapter 4 articulates curricular, instructional, and assessment principles that follow from this changed starting point. Finally, Chapter 5 lays out plausible steps we can take to start over.

ACKNOWLEDGMENTS

Books do not get written by just one person and this one is no exception. I want to thank my students who have all pushed me to think deeply about education and the practices therein. My colleagues in the Warner Graduate School of Education and Human Development, Raffaella Borasi, Kevin Meuwissen, Jeff Choppin, Ed Brockenbrough, Nancy Ares, Mary Jane Curry, Julia White, Jayne Lammers, David Hursh, Martha Mock, April Luehmann, Susan Hetherington, Brian Brent, and Andrew Wall, listened to several of the ideas in this volume and gave me wonderful feedback. Thanks for such a great work environment. Thanks especially to Jeff Choppin for his careful reading of an early first draft. Thank you to Julia White for reading my discussions about children and youth with disability labels. Courtney Hanny and Burke Scarbrough contributed important insights to later drafts for which I shall always be grateful. I thank Mary Jane Curry for her careful final read through. And thanks to all the teachers I have worked with over the years, both new and veteran, who have taught me what it means to teach and to authentically learn. I am grateful to Naomi Silverman at Routledge for trusting me. I thank Kris Gutiérrez, my friend and mentor, who agreed to write the Foreword, and whose keen intellect has shaped my own thinking. Finally, I am incredibly grateful for the love and support of my husband Morris Smith and my children, Anna, Eric, and Marcus.

1

FED UP WITH TINKERING

Imagine if schools were different than they are now[1]—equitable and fair for all children and youth. Imagine if we started with an assumption of equality of intelligence and saw all people as important and valuable contributors to learning endeavors. Imagine if everybody counted and that, by everybody, we meant *everybody*. Imagine if teachers and students were both learners in just and equitable communities where we all worked together to use what we produce, or produse,[2] knowledge, and make meaning. Imagine.

Can you imagine children and youth (and community members, teachers, administrators, parents) drawing from a range of institutions (schools, museums, businesses, social service agencies) to solve local problems or issues all while produsing knowledge in the service of a common good that they themselves have constructed? Imagine a space where learners co-construct their learning, their understandings of the sociopolitical problems at play, the potential solutions, and their consequences. Imagine that outdated autonomous[3] school knowledges are transformed to be relevant in real communities and for social justice ends. While we would find some classrooms where these things are happening, they are not systemic.

What sort of ontological changes would we need to move away from assumptions of inequality to assumptions of equality? How might we implement the transformation needed to accomplish these imaginings? A lot of things would need to change to make these imaginings real. Given the years of reform tried already perhaps it is time to start over with new assumptions. None of the past or current reforms have resulted in a just and equitable education system, and a just and equitable system should be a minimum goal. Dramatic change seems especially important now that new technologies and their resultant new practices have radically changed the way humans learn, interact, and produse knowledge in contemporary times. Schools are moving dangerously toward irrelevance in ways that make starting over the only viable option.

While not a script for action, this book does articulate theoretical, curricular, pedagogical, and assessment *principles* to start over in education in order to adequately respond to and shape radical changes in ways of knowing and being associated with new technologies and knowledge production practices. I argue that schools are in what Bruns (2008) calls "casual collapse" because they have not responded to the profound changes in knowing and being that have occurred globally in the twenty-first century. Working within the system as it is currently will not work to prevent this collapse. We need to start over with different ontological and epistemological foundations and robust theories that help explain new social and power relations. We need to assume equality rather than inequality of intelligence (Rancière, 1991). We, educational researchers, practitioners, parents, community members, and children and youth, need to understand what it means when *everybody comes* (Shirky, 2008) and when *everybody counts,* because not to do so will maintain current and deepening inequities (Darling-Hammond, 2010; Gee, 2013a).

There are three main threads to my argument that we need to start over. One, schools are limited and outdated in the models of learning they rely on, especially when compared with models of learning we find elsewhere. Two, schools do not serve the interests of the majority of children and youth in schools today, privileged or otherwise. Moreover, the lack of attention to new communicative practices results in inequities and damages children, especially with the current obsessive focus on test scores. And three, schools are oriented around producing/sorting worker-citizens whereas they should be organized to equitably produce socially engaged produsers. Given these points, we need to start over with new ontological and epistemological assumptions rather than tinker with the current system. In what follows I offer more detailed explanations of these three strands of my argument.

What We Already Know: Schools Are Outdated

In their current state, schools are irrelevant to the meaning making and knowledge production needed in contemporary times. Schools are based on an outdated, scarcity production model of curriculum, instruction, and assessment that is grounded in traditional business economics and that does not respond to changes in skills and practices needed to participate in a global world. This is not a new argument, however. Similar arguments were made in the early twentieth century during industrialization. Calls for changing schools to accommodate a changing world of work rang through the public discourse on education. I am not making a "change so we can have more efficient workers" argument here. My main argument is that we need to change schools so that they are equitable and just, not so that they produce workers who can compete in a global marketplace.

Part of how we make schools equitable and just has to do with ensuring they are relevant and meaningful to children and youth in *all* communities. One place where schools have become outdated is by not taking into account the changed and changing practices associated with Internet communication technologies and social media. They have missed the valuable learning and development going on in those spaces. Furthermore, authentic acknowledgment and use of culturally varied ways of knowing and being (Gutiérrez & Rogoff, 2003; King, 1994; Ladson-Billings, 1995; Lee, 2001; Moll, Amanti, Neff, & Gonzales, 1992) occurring in those spaces is also lost on schools.

In fact, de Alba, Gonzáles-Gaudiano, Lankshear, and Peters (2000, p. 9) argue that "our curricula are becoming overwhelmed by practices of diagnosis, intervention, and remediation grounded not merely in 'basic skills,' but in *old and outmoded* forms of basic skills" (emphasis in original). The basic skills we need are not simply those used to fill a workforce, but to engage a dynamic generation of sophisticated children and youth in knowledge production. Recently there has been a call in the research on teaching for high-level content knowledge that echoes the call to move beyond reductionist notions about what counts as basic:

> Business, government, and educational leaders assert that across grade levels and subject matters, all kinds of students should be engaged in cognitively challenging tasks in school and should be treated as people who can think and who know how to do things. They believe students should learn, not only to read and calculate, but also to analyze texts and tables and to write in ways that communicate the results of their analysis, providing evidence for their conclusions.
>
> *(Partnership for 21st Century Skills, 2007,*
> *cited in Lambert, Boerst, & Graziani, 2011, p. 1361)*

Additionally, models of production/consumption imported from old business practices no longer apply, since this binary has shifted to produsage models (Bruns, 2008; Lankshear & Knobel, 2011). Fordist models of production used an input–output model in which the "public's" only role was as passive consumers of goods designed and built by others. We had no role in the design of goods or services beyond embodying the "demand" (as in the supply/demand binary), to use the language of economists. Education simply imported this model into the design and implementation of curriculum in ways that have led to students and teachers being positioned as passive consumers, which seriously underestimates their capabilities (de Certeau, 1984), and does not serve them well. We could say that assessment equals the demand of economists and that students (and taxpayers) are positioned as passive consumers. Building on principles of efficiency and productivity imported from industry, the "users," (students) only role was to have needs that the expert (curriculum developer) measured, filled, and measured again. The user-only role positioned students and teachers as unequal in relation to outside curriculum "experts" and as needing instruction. A counter to this hegemonic economic model would build local and sustainable economies that educate people to think in complex and critical ways that can contribute to the construction of an equitable and just society.

Traditional models of schooling operate on the factory model (Kliebard, 2004) in which production efficiency is the priority and which focuses on linearity and conformity (Robinson, 2010b). From this perspective, knowledge exists as a static entity outside of human action that floats around or that exists in textbooks and curriculum materials waiting to be discovered. The materials themselves are containers from which learners extract knowledge. In effect, the belief is that textbooks, not teachers, teach (Shannon, 1989). Teachers, or better yet curriculum experts, take the knowledge and break it down into component parts, sequence it according to developmental (stage) theories of learning or disciplinary logics, and insert tests/rewards at pre-determined points. In this traditional input–output model (see Figure 1.1), knowledge is put into empty heads, and it is assumed that we can determine whether someone has learned something through administering a standardized test. However, some educational research has pointed to a more local vision of knowledge production that articulates the use of local curriculum teams such as those I discuss in this book, rather than outside entities "giving" curriculum (cf. Bigum, 2002; Facer, 2011; Lewis, Perry, & Murata, 2006).

In current times, further assumptions about knowledge production stemming from this input–output model have been brought to bear on schools. Indeed the factory model has become hegemonic. Current accountability discourses, for example, operate from the assumption that teachers are not adequately skilled to teach, so they need increasingly detailed and prescriptive curriculum packages that will teach for them (Apple, 1990; Shannon, 1989). Furthermore, students

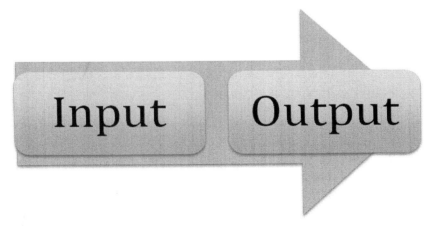

FIGURE 1.1 Outdated model

are assumed to be empty vessels that need filling by packaged curricula designed by "experts" (Freire, 1970). The only role available to students is recipient of external expertise—the ultimate in inequality according to Rancière (see Chapter 2). As the child realizes that her intelligence is not equal, she takes on the role of mourner. She is always in need, never in a position to be expert at something, hence the need to mourn. Anything other than the old school traditional "transmission" model of education, such as collaborative learning in inquiry communities, is considered with disdain to be a fad and can thus be dismissed (Kohn, 1999).

[handwritten margin notes: Knowledge not valued / worthy/correct]

In other fields, such as communication and economics, Shirky (2008, 2010), Bruns (2008), and Godin (2008) have articulated ideas about the changed and changing nature of society, ideas that focus on what is different now that everyone can participate. Internet sites such as Wikipedia, open source computer languages such as Linux, and the mass participation afforded by social networking technologies are consistent with what educational researchers from a social practice perspective of content knowledge and learning have been saying for decades about the social construction of knowledge (Cole, 1996). By bringing these views together, we can reconceptualize contexts for learning that focus more on what it means to participate in authentic practices in the twenty-first century than on memorizing and testing decontextualized skills.

Research in these and other fields has shown that profound shifts are happening in society in the everyday multimodal, multi-authored digital communication practices that enable formerly passive audiences to shift toward a participatory convergence culture,[4] transforming the social relations between production and consumption (Jenkins, 2006) into what Bruns (2008) calls produsage or the simultaneous use and construction of knowledge. Ignoring these shifts has made schools largely irrelevant to the children, youth, and young adults across diverse communities who are participating in these practices in unprecedented ways (boyd, 2008; Gee, 2004, 2010; Ito et al., 2010; Lankshear & Knobel, 2010). These technologies have disassembled and rearranged old technologies and their associated subjectivities in ways that call for a profound rethinking of what schools do and what (and whose) purposes they serve (Peters & Burbules, 2004). The formerly closed space of the classroom is now open to futures as yet unwritten. By not paying attention to these changes and by allowing the narrative about those changes to go unexamined (Facer, 2011), schools will continue to have futures written for them instead of proactively taking an authorship role.

[handwritten margin note: Produsage]

In produsage models common in contemporary life outside of school, the producer/consumer binary is disrupted. "We the people," formerly known as the audience, now can talk back (and to each other) in powerful ways (Shirky, 2008). We do not wait for experts to tell us what we want or need; we make it ourselves. We evaluate whether it is good or bad, and if it is bad we fix it. We use what we produse and all this is done in record time. Bruns (2008) cites Wikipedia as a classic example of this process. In Wikipedia we see the collaborative, user-led produsage of a globally diverse human knowledge base that remains fluidly in production. When I mention this point to the teachers I work with, they immediately cite examples of false information on Wikipedia as evidence of its unreliability. True, but what has also happened is self-correction. "We the people" have found ways to stop the deliberate contamination of what constitutes a world knowledge base and produse a reliable resource for what humans know. If schools operated with a produsage mindset such as Wikipedia's, curriculum and assessment would be constructed locally in collaborative activity. Collaborators would include students, teachers, administrators, parents, and community members. What counted as evidence of success would not be efficiency measures, but use value. Shifting away from outdated input–output models is crucial to the starting over process I advocate for in this book.

What is frustrating is that we, education researchers and high-quality change agent[5] teachers, know more meaningful ways to construct schooling because we have been researching and writing about just such scenarios for decades (Noguera, 2013; Rose, 2009). We (educational researchers and practitioners) know a lot about how to construct authentic and relevant contexts for learning, but what we know is not generally present in schools today, except for the few spaces where change agent teachers and administrators work against the grain. We know, for example, that you cannot do reform from the top down, outside in (Darling-Hammond, 2010; Tyack & Cuban, 1995). Yet governments, both state and federal, continue to impose a particular type of reform based on narrow modernism implemented from the outside which districts implement from the top down. What does it mean that "down" is always directed at teachers? When grassroots, teacher-driven reforms such as Whole Language (Goodman, 1987) surfaced and began to take hold, they were squashed vehemently and even banned. With the current focus on testing, we know that children and youth do not count except as data points in the form of standardized test scores (Spring, 2012). Now those same scores will shape teacher evaluations (USDOE, 2012b).

What we know about content and learning is extensive yet tends not to be present in the everyday life of schools or in teacher preparation. In literacy studies, for example, we know from Gee (2011) and Lankshear and Knobel (2011) among others that new digital literacies with a new ethos[6] are predominant in the everyday lives of children and youth but that schools have not figured out how to address these, choosing instead to focus on outdated conceptions of literacy as neutral skills separated from their contexts of use and relations of power (Larson, 2007). Teacher preparation institutions often reflect autonomous models of literacy (Street, 1995) and are not preparing new teachers for these ʔew practices. The focus on Internet communication technologies in schools ies almost exclusively on technologies that see children as data points to be ᵐaged (Spring, 2012) or in ways to make outdated practices more efficient. affordances of new technologies to shape and change what and how we know is intentionally bypassed by the corporations that market data management software packages and glossy curriculum tools.

We also know that the learning theories emerging from studies of video games and social networking technologies are more robust than those in use in most schools. Children's and youth's learning in these environments is fluid, supported on a just-in-time and as needed basis, and driven by their interests, friendships, and desires (Gee, 2004, 2013b; Ito et al., 2010). Gee (2004, 2007) has shown that complex and authentic learning occurs when children and youth play difficult video games. He introduces the idea of affinity spaces to explain the social relations that develop from shared interest in these spaces. Traditional identity categories such as race, class, gender, ability, linguistic practice, and sexual orientation fade when the grouping is around interest and desire. Ito et al. (2010) have shown that youth spend time in these spaces developing and using complex communicative practices that have not been documented before.

This research is consistent with Vygotskian and neo-Vygotskian theories of learning such as those found in communities of learners (Rogoff, 1994), communities of practice (Lave & Wenger, 1991), and Gutiérrez and Rogoff's (2003) ideas about repertoires of practice that help us move away from monolithic views of learning, culture, and cultural groups. From this perspective, learning occurs through participation in culturally valued activities and practices. As Ito et al. (2010) have shown, children and youth are valuing different activities and practices than we dreamed possible just a few years ago. Furthermore, we know that if we take video games or other digital practices into schools without first transforming the ethos of schools, we will destroy whatever it is that makes them attractive to students in the first place (Gee, 2004). Street (1995) would call this "pedagogization" or the transformation of anything meaningful or authentic into autonomous definitions of knowledge wherein knowledge is understood to be context independent. This decontextualization limits possibilities for meaning making to that which is determined by school. The assumption that knowledge is autonomous and neutral misunderstands how knowledge is produced and used in contemporary times. Furthermore, it assumes inequality of intelligence that results in the pedagogical myth that instruction requires explanation (Rancière, 1991).

Current policy makers apparently only look to the research that confirms and replicates traditional transmission (input–output) conceptions of schooling because they do not want to jeopardize profits or, more generally, alter the status quo of power relations (Britzman, 2003). By the singular focus on profit, I mean both political profit for themselves and economic profit for corporations and businesses upon which they rely for funding and political support. They are the same "men in the back room" that have always been there, maintaining their privilege (Mills, 2000). I acknowledge Foucault's (1978) point that power is everywhere and his caution not to look for specific entities. However, to not name the people and their intentions behind these efforts at control perpetuates

[handwritten margin note: Who have been arguing with?]

the problem of unjust and inequitable schooling. Corporations and businesses who have a stake in garnering profit from education appear to not be interested in the kinds of authentic teaching and learning that educational researchers cited in this book have been arguing for, but instead focus on preparing workers for economic competition in a global marketplace as the purpose of schooling (Common Core, 2012a). Spring (2012) calls these individuals the "global shadow elite" who work in the shadows to fulfill their own profit motives.

Children and Youth Are Not Being Well-served: Standardization and Obsessive Testing Causes Damage

> It is our continuing comfort with profound inequality that is the Achilles heel of American education.
>
> (Darling-Hammond, 2010, p. 8)

There is a growing apartheid in schools, with concentrations of high poverty and children and youth from non-dominant groups coming to schools that are in deplorable condition (Darling-Hammond, 2010; Kozol, 2006; USDOE, 2013). Very little has changed, as Darling-Hammond suggests, with regard to continued inequality and in spite of reforms aimed at ameliorating these injustices. The racist, classist, ableist, linguistic, and sexist hegemony of the current system and of related ideas about intelligence and exclusion have contributed to the current state of inequality. The stakes are high indeed.

But the stakes are different than the stakes attached to a test score. Instead, it is a battle for survival. It is a crisis when children are being harmed, and they are. They are harmed by test driven pedagogies rooted in deficit ideologies about who poor children and children from non-dominant groups[7] are and of what they are capable. I have seen children slump in their chairs when teachers squash their ideas or criticize their use of language, for example (Irvine & Larson, 2007). We tend not to see the damage so much in White middle- and upper-class children and youth because of their tendency to score well, because of out-of-school supports and additional resources in their home communities. I am *not* saying that poor children and children from non-dominant groups do not get support at home, because they do. But that support is not necessarily the support that is demanded by the currently narrow cultural focus of schooling. This lack of recognition of who they are and what they can bring to learning, in effect, "kills" them. Middle- and upper-class White kids are not "killed" in schools but damage is being done nonetheless: damage to critical, innovative, and creative thinking (Robinson, 2010a). By critical I do not mean the ability to analyze or synthesize information as measured on standardized test rubrics. I mean the ability to deconstruct power relations evident in texts (broadly defined) and uncover inequalities in order to rectify them (Janks, 2010; Morrell, 2008). This is definitely not happening in most schools. Frankly, not even the generic definition of "critical" is happening in schools. Pre-packaged, test driven pedagogies have stamped that out. In literacy education, so-called "basic" skills such as comprehension have become the ability to retell a story; "understanding" in an authentic sense of textual interpretation and critique does not seem to count at all. It is difficult for students to understand when texts are abridged or shortened to the point of no longer making any sense, as is often done in basal readers and anthologies (Larson, 2007). All of these things do a disservice to children and youth across communities.

Classrooms remain the same teacher-centered, authoritarian spaces now as they were when Goodlad (1984) conducted his classic study (Kohn, 1999). With recent policy initiatives such as Race to the Top (USDOE, 2012b), even with the flexibility waivers, not only have we maintained that unjust system, we have moved to an obsessive focus on standardization and testing that produces deeper inequities. As the recent Equity and Education Commission (USDOE, 2013, p. 15) report states:

> No other developed nation has inequities nearly as deep or systemic; no other developed nation has, despite some efforts to the contrary, so thoroughly stacked the odds against so many of its children.

How has it become acceptable for these inequities to exist? We have lost our way somewhere along the line.

I often wonder why "we the people" are not angrier about it. The achievement gap has increased since social movements of the 1960s were reversed with Reagan–Bush era politics, and that gap has now stabilized (NCES, 2011a, 2011b). Resegregation has occurred as middle- and upper-class Whites, Blacks, and Latina/os left urban settings for the suburbs (Baum-Snow & Lutz, 2011; Orfield, 2001; Tatum, 2007). English learners continue to be disadvantaged while trying to figure out the U.S. educational system (Ngo, 2006). Immigrant and refugee children are more likely to struggle with school and drop out than their native born peers (NCES, 2008). An obsessive focus on achievement on standardized tests has produced cheating (Guisbond, Neill, & Schaeffer, 2012), damage to children, and reductionist curricula (Au, 2007). This collateral damage established by research (Nichols & Berliner, 2007) is simply not acceptable. These inequities cannot be allowed and must be stopped, even reversed.

It has been long documented that people with disability labels have been excluded from general education settings and that there is tremendous over-representation of African Americans in special education, which also causes damage (Artiles, 2001; Blanchett, 2006; Erevelles, 2000; Ferri & Connor, 2005). In spite of legislation that calls for students with disability labels to be educated alongside their non-disabled peers to the maximum extent possible, these children and youth remain marginalized across the educational spectrum (Hayman, 1998).

Beyond the research documentation, I can personally attest to this situation because I have a biracial son with a severe disability. He continues to be educated in self-contained settings because I refuse to allow him to be further damaged by an inadequate general education system that will not accommodate his needs. When by the end of kindergarten he was placed in a closet (yes a converted closet!) with a paraprofessional to keep him away from his peers, I said "no more" and pulled him out. Apparently, the law does not matter for some children, mine included.

To be sure, on the ground in some classrooms around the United States there are everyday celebrations of authentic teaching and learning and vibrant knowledge production goes on in these rooms. But, often, that celebration and production stops at the classroom door and has to be done subversively for fear of censure of the teachers for using innovative pedagogies. We have allowed external forces—neoliberal, non-educators—to break the school culture in the name of accountability. Accountable to whom? Why? Whose purposes are being served by this reductionist focus? I argue that corporate purposes are taking precedence over authentic teaching and learning and that this process is damaging children.

Furthermore, research has shown for a long time that standardization and standardized testing harms children (Kohn, 1999; McNeil, 2000; Nichols & Berliner, 2007) and only captures the cognitive dimension of human learning and development. Frankly, standardized testing does not even capture the cognitive dimension that well (Kohn, 1999) as it only "tests" particular ways of knowing (reading and writing). Students who "know" differently do not have the opportunity to show what they know. No Child Left Behind's focus on a single test score has failed to narrow the achievement gap, discounts the role of poverty on school participation, narrows the curriculum, and promotes teaching to the test (Au, 2007; Duncan & Murnane, 2011; Guisbond, Neill, & Shaeffer, 2012; Hout & Elliott, 2011; NCES, 2011a, 2011b; Popham, 2004; Shepard, 1990). Nichols and Berliner (2007) have comprehensively outlined the literature on standardized testing to conclude that high-stakes testing undermines the educational system; therefore I will not summarize it here. Suffice it to say that we know from research that high-stakes standardized testing does damage and should not be used. U.S. Secretary of Education Arne Duncan's (2013) recent statement that current problems with testing should result in better tests strikes me as an extreme misunderstanding of the problem at hand. "Better" damage? It just does not make sense and is clearly the wrong direction if we want meaning making to be a part of a just and equitable education system.

Competitive achievement discourses and assessment/accountability rhetorics that use test scores as the measure of achievement remain hegemonically in the background as how we define "success". By achievement discourses, I mean the language, rhetoric, and practices around achievement as test score. We are in an age of accountability to be sure, but just because that is the current discourse does not mean it should be. Educational researchers know a great deal about authentic assessments that are simply ignored by the "business" of education. Yet, we have let outside business interests overtake the work of educating our young. And business is only interested in profit and efficiency, not in equitable education for all children and youth. "Ultimately, the *goals* of business are not the same as those of educators and parents . . . When business thinks about schools, its agenda is driven by what will maximize its profitability, not necessarily by what is in the best interest of students" (Kohn, 1999, p. 15). Big money interests, including big philanthropy money like the Gates Foundation (2012), enter the conversation on education unimpeded and impose what they think is best. They are not educators or education researchers. They cherry-pick the research that will support their argument and they do not understand the complexities of research in general or education research specifically.

Schools maintain status quo achievement discourses by continuing to claim that higher achievement is what counts as success. Most literature and news reports on schools these days talk obsessively about "achievement" as though it is an end point in education. When we read closely, we can see that instead of accomplishing something, achievement refers only to a standardized test score. Very little public discourse focuses on learning. As Kohn (1999, p. 21) suggests, "A *preoccupation with achievement* is not only different from, but often detrimental to, a focus on learning" (emphasis in original). This fetishizing of achievement leads to competitive school cultures, superficial thinking, and an anti-learning environment (Kohn, 1999) in which what gets learned is of less value than a score on a test. It is this single-minded focus on the score as proxy for achievement that partly grounds my argument that we need to start over rather than tinker with a broken system.

No Child Left Behind claims that narrowing the achievement gap is one reason for standardized testing. However, gains achieved in terms of narrowing the achievement gap, or what Dixon-Román (2010) refers to as the economy of difference, as a result of social and educational reforms of the 1960s and 1970s were reversed by conservative policy elite's decisions in the Reagan–Bush eras and their focus on outcomes (standardized tests) rather than inputs such as high quality teacher education and professional development (Darling-Hammond, 2010). The inequities have accumulated over the years to result in what Ladson-Billings (2006) has called our educational debt, or the accumulation of damage over time. Dixon-Román's (2010, p. 96) concept of the economy of difference articulates how "a market of scarcity of the various forms of resources meaningful for the development of situated optimal human potential" produces this debt. High-stakes standardized testing capitalizes on the scarcity model to exclude vast majorities of poor children and children and youth from non-dominant groups, including people with disability labels and English learners. This situation is simply intolerable if we value our children and youth. Again, it makes me wonder why people are not angrier about the lack of equity and justice in schoolir

Traditional Purposes Reflect an Unproductive Binary of Worker/Citizen

Historically, the purposes of education have included preparation for "complete living" (Spencer, 1860), development of character (Herbart, 1904), preparation for the "adult world" (Bobbitt, 1918), societal improvement and democratic participation (Dewey, 1938), humanization of the social order (Bode, 1927), preparation to participate in social change (Counts, 1932), bringing learners in contact with reality (MacDonald, 1975) (cited in Pinar, 1995), and producing moral people with mental discipline (Du Bois, 1903/2002) (see Figure 1.2). None of these historical purposes has resulted in equitable and just education for all children. Current public schooling has exacerbated disparities along race, class, gender, sexual orientation, linguistic, and ability lines through a narrow focus on test scores (Guisbond, Neill, & Schaeffer, 2012; McNeil, 2000). People with disability labels, particularly those with severe disabilities, are more excluded than ever, especially when ability intersects with race (Artiles, 2001).

Consistent across traditional versions of the purpose of schooling is the binary notion that schools prepare youth for work and/or for citizenship. Variously, and according to political whims of the time, one or the other of these purposes takes precedence, though it is unclear the extent to which any aim has actually been accomplished (Larson, 2013). The classic example of a swing in emphasis between worker/citizen was the U.S. reaction to the launch of Sputnik in 1957.

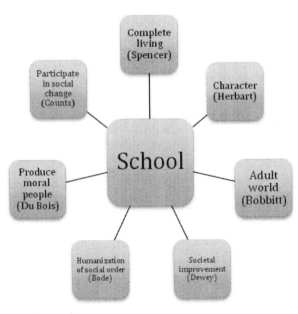

torical purposes

Before the launch, some of Dewey's concepts of relevance and experiential learning were being implemented in schools (Kliebard, 2004; McNeil, 1990). With Sputnik, however, a rabid return to a narrow definition of the "basics" followed with calls for winning the space race through U.S. innovations in science and math. New curricula were designed and implemented, which failed miserably. The social movements of the 1960s saw a shift back to meaning and citizenship; however, the 1983 release of *A Nation At Risk* with its fear-based calls for economic competition snapped us back to the "basics" which we are currently facing. Goals 2000, No Child Left Behind (NCLB), and Race To The Top (RTTT), and now the Common Core Learning Standards, are extensions of this basic skills backlash, but they have added high-stakes accountability into the mix. None of these changes in emphasis between producing workers in a globally competitive marketplace or citizens in a democracy has resulted in a just and equitable education system. We need a new purpose that privileges equity and social justice.

The purposes of schooling exist on a spectrum that ranges from, and vacillates between, maintaining a competitive market edge (building workers) and educating a democratic citizenry (building a citizen). As I mentioned, one end of the spectrum focuses on skills for the workforce. The other end of the spectrum is the goal to produce democratic citizens (Biesta, 2009). One could argue that "they" do not really want everyone to achieve this, especially given Thomas Jefferson's (1784/1954) idea that schools should weed out the unwashed masses and produce political leaders of a particular sort. Jefferson simply instantiated existing stratifications to protect the elite and maintain the status quo. Traces of this weeding out ideology remain in how schools are stratified along race, class, gender, sexual orientation, linguistic, and ability lines. The same dominant group (White, middle-, and upper-class) gets the goods (college, financial security, etc.) that society has to offer and the same oppressed groups get left out. All attempts to make learning more authentic and meaningful for all children might have some impact for White, wealthy and middle-class children and youth, but poor children and children and youth from non-dominant groups rarely see these changes. More than likely they see increasingly reductionist curricula and pedagogy (Au, 2007; Duncan & Murnane, 2011; Hout & Eliott, 2011; Saltman, 2012). As Gee has stated, "School is bad for all kids, white kids just get As for it" (personal communication, 2009). "Citizenship" only appears to be available for some.

Why Now?

I am writing this book because I just cannot take it anymore. Enough is enough. Current inequities should not be tolerated in a society in which all people are created equal. Tinkering with the current U.S. educational system from within for the past 200 years has not provided a just[8] and equitable education for all children. We need to start over. If schools do not respond to the profound sociocultural changes that have occurred in human interaction and meaning making in the twenty-first century, they are in danger of becoming more irrelevant than ever. Very little has changed regarding just and equitable education over the years in spite of repeated cycles of reform and calls for change. In fact, things are worse than ever. We are increasing inequities with the current standardization and accountability movement and its associated constellation of mandates. Researchers often refer to the pendulum swing of reforms that teachers just wait out. I see it rather as a vicious cycle or a spinning wheel that is stuck in the mud. We accelerate more and it only digs us further into the mud. I argue in this book that we need to get out of the mud altogether.

We, educational researchers and practitioners, have been trying to make an impact on these inequities for over 100 years and nothing has worked. The dominant model for the purpose of schooling as economic competition, now globally focused, remains like a deep ocean under insignificant waves of feeble attempts at transformation. I argue that part of why we have not been able to change the system to be more socially just and relevant to today's children and youth is the entrenchment of power elites in crucial decision-making positions and their desire to keep things the way they are—they are the primary beneficiaries of reductionist curriculum and accountability systems, especially since "they" tend to be the ones who own the companies that produce the textbooks and testing materials and who stand to profit from mandating these packages in federal legislation (Larson, 2007; Spring, 2012).

Who are these power elites (cf. Mills, 2000)? Tyack and Cuban (1995) describe what they call policy elites as those people who manage the economy, have privileged access to the media and to politicians, educational leaders (e.g., university faculty, state superintendents who are often not educators themselves), and people who control charitable and political foundations. I would call these same people power elites, agreeing with Tyack and Cuban that they are the same groups of people today as they have been since the beginning of U.S. public education. I would add textbook publishers to the mix and politicians themselves, not just those who have privileged access to them. Spring's (2012) thorough analysis of who these people are might help us to combat their unearned influence.

The Reading First legislation mandated under No Child Left Behind is one example of how these elites exchange power and how they work to maintain control while earning a profit. Reading First was designed to provide early reading intervention for kindergarten through second grade by using scientifically based reading instruction. Research has now shown clearly that Reading First was a failure and that its entrenchment in U.S. literacy policy was a result of the relationship between the McGraws of McGraw-Hill publishing and the Bush family, and that it was not based on adequate research (Coles, 2003; SDOIG, 2006). The "good old boys" network was at play and McGraw-Hill made substantial profit from being named as *the way* to meet No Child Left Behind reading benchmarks in early childhood (Coles 2003; Osborn, 2007). The business of testing has been a key factor in how we ended up with this testing obsession (Altwerger & Strauss, 2002; Leitsyyna, 2007).

Alliances between textbook publishers and various levels of government through implementation of educational mandates and increasing reliance on high-stakes standardized tests have resulted in narrow, selective, and minimalist education goals that facilitate control over educational content and processes. These alliances have silenced discussion about other possible goals for education (Larson, Allen, & Osborn, 2010). Particular views, those of the power elite, are thus reified in education through these strategic partnerships between "old family friends" in high ranking political positions and CEOs of major corporations and publishing houses (Osborn, 2007; Spring, 2012). Most of these elite power brokers operate invisibly to the general public. "Like the normalizing gaze of the examination, the disciplinary power of curriculum is exercised through its invisibility; invisibility achieved through a focus on sameness, and supposed neutrality, which legitimates and may even disguise the exercise of power" (Larson, Allen, & Osborn, 2010, p. 372). The disguise must be revealed and dismantled so that "we the people" can take back our schools.

Researchers have been making the argument that we need to rethink schooling (Christensen, Hansen, Peterson, Schlessman, & Watson, 2012; Collins & Halverson, 2009; Darling-Hammond, 2010; Egan, 2008). Mostly, they make solid and convincing arguments for working within the system to change it. However, they tend to remain focused on "achievement" as the principal indicator of success, even when there are social justice ends. They define achievement along a continuum from narrow skills-based views (e.g., scores on high-stakes standardized tests) to broader definitions that include assessments that measure inquiry thinking. The purpose of schooling that they articulate remains located in the worker/citizen binary that has become hegemonic in U.S. schools but has not resulted in a just and equitable system. Achievement discourses are linked to these notions of building effective citizens (inquiry thinking) or efficient workers (high-stakes standardized tests). I argue that holding achievement static along with traditional purposes of schooling will not result in just and equitable schools needed to produce the kinds of knowledge used in the twenty-first century. We need a more complex understanding. We need to start over with new ontological and epistemological footings.

As educational researchers we have spent our time working in the leeway, writing research articles and attending conferences where we hear the same arguments over and over. One consequence has been the continued focus on the connection between the discourses of achievement and deficit discourses (e.g., Valencia, 2010), and the tying together of broader issues of deficit notions of children to the "scientific" construction of curricula. The link between deficit ideologies and curriculum has been a defining part of U.S. education for over a century.

Another consequence may be that the social contract of school has been irrevocably broken by these hegemonic instrumentalist discourses that privilege the rational subject of modernism (Biesta, 2009). No Child Left Behind (USDOE, 2012a) and Race to the Top (USDOE, 2012b) undermine that contract by reinforcing the flawed assumptions underlying the current system—that intelligence is unequal. The current high-stakes testing environment does damage children. Just because it is the law does not make it right. Many, many laws have been just plain wrong and do not result in a just and equitable system. The emphasis on achievement and achievement scores, and new policies that link student test scores to teacher evaluation, is just plain wrong.

Why Start Over?

Simply put, children, youth, and teachers are being hurt. Working within the system has so far not remedied this situation, rather things are getting worse. Now with the Annual Professional Performance Review (APPR) added into the mix, things are becoming much worse than we can imagine for teachers struggling to do the right thing for their students. Furthermore, the hegemonic purposes of schooling are no longer viable, especially for those children and youth who have been disenfranchised from the beginning. Researchers, scholars, educators, policy makers, teachers, and administrators need to fundamentally rethink, redefine, and reshape the purposes of schooling, their understanding of knowledge production/use (produsage) and learning, and pedagogical practices in order to authentically participate in the conversation that our children and youth are already having (Shirky, 2008). Ignoring the shifts in everyday multimodal, multi-authored digital communication practices, for example, has made schools largely irrelevant to the children, youth, and young adults who are participating in these practices in unprecedented ways. Formerly passive audiences are no longer restrained by one-to-many participation structures. The shift toward a participatory convergence culture has transformed communication into many-to-many participation structures in which the social relations between production and consumption are blurred, if not erased (Jenkins, 2006; Jenkins, Ford, & Green, 2013; Shirky, 2008). Knowledge production and meaning making are now occurring more authentically outside of the formal educational system, including private and charter schools. Children and youth are not "playing" at something that they will grow out of; these *are* the language, literacy, and knowledge production practices now. We must recognize this shift or risk continued irrelevance.

If society wants schooling and education to play a meaningful role in shaping our children and youth, in knowledge production and meaning making, and in producing justice and equity, schooling needs to move past irrelevance. We need a dramatic shift in how we define knowledge production (from transmission to produsage), learning (from rote to collaborative participation), teaching (from all-knowing to collaborative learners), and where we think learning happens

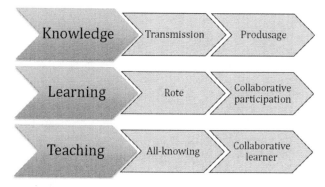

FIGURE 1.3 Changes we need

(handwritten margin note: Why does this all need to occur in school?)

(see Figure 1.3). We need to re-imagine schools in radical ways, ways that focus on agency and expansive learning (Gutierrez & Larson, 2007). Children and youth (and community members, teachers, parents, administrators) could work to solve local problems/issues all while produsing knowledge in the service of the common good in ways that produce equity and justice.

Thus we need a new starting place wherein all intelligence is equal and in which everyone counts. This book articulates a possible path to equity and justice in schooling by making the case for radical equality in education. This first chapter has articulated some of the reasons why we need to start over. Chapter 2 outlines the ontological position that all intelligence is equal and describes a different theoretical framing that follows from this position. I use two main examples, one an urban classroom and one an urban community transformation initiative, to provide concrete visioning of the possibilities of this new ontological and theoretical framing. Chapter 3 establishes that the traditional purposes of schooling are outmoded and argues that the purpose of school should be *to facilitate human learning, meaning making, and knowledge production toward a just and equitable education for all.* In Chapter 4, I put forward potential principles for rethinking curriculum, instruction, and assessment that are grounded in the framework articulated in Chapter 2, combined with poststructural curriculum theories. Chapter 5 outlines a plausible plan for action.

Notes

1 Cf. Kozol (2006, 2012a, 2012b) for detailed documentation of inequities in U.S. education.
2 Produsage will be explained in detail in Chapter 2. In brief, it means that we have shifted from a consumer model of knowledge production to a produsage model in which users use what they produce, or produse.
3 Street (1995) distinguishes between autonomous, or skills-based, views of knowledge, literacy in particular, and ideological or situated, contextualized views.

4 Jenkins (2006) discusses convergence culture as spaces where people gather and merge practices from multiple spaces.

5 By change agent teachers I am referring to those teachers who understand teaching and learning to be socially constructed and who fight against the damages that the standardization movement has done to authentic purposes of schooling.

6 Lankshear and Knobel (2011) refer to new literacies as having both new technical stuff (e.g., hardware and bandwidth) and new ethos stuff (e.g., new ways of being and doing with new technical stuff).

7 By non-dominant, I mean children and youth from non-White, non-middle/upper class, and non-native English speaking backgrounds. I would also include Lesbian Gay Bisexual Transgendered (LGBT) youth and people with disability labels in this group.

8 I define just as that which is morally good, rather than the legal focus of legally correct. I define equity as freedom from the consequences of bias or prejudice and, following Gutiérrez (2012), as fairness not sameness. Following Fielding and Moss (2011), I argue that a just society provides equal access to the material and social means to construct positive futures.

[handwritten annotations] Basically those that are anti standardization that have different ideas about education + teaching. Why Teach? — Content expert? Just proves you've been filled. Care for childern development

2
FROM AN EQUITABLE
STARTING PLACE

Do schools contribute to justice and equity in the contemporary U.S.? Have they paid attention to changes going on around them? I argue here that they are not paying attention to a changed and changing society, but they should. The world is a very different place now that we have mass collaboration and interconnectivity via the Internet (Rheingold, 2002; Shirky, 2008). Not paying attention to these changes has led to schooling's irrelevance for contemporary children and youth across communities. Furthermore, by not using these technologies in schools in authentic ways (e.g., using the new ethos), current gaps in usage will widen, contributing to furthering inequity. Thus, my claim that schools do not currently help to build a just and equitable society, yet they should. Justice and equity in school and society should be a baseline goal of education. I will explain these points in more detail in this chapter, followed by an articulation of new ontological and epistemological views that might help us move toward equity and justice in U.S. education.

It has become clear recently that schools have largely ignored the profound shift in everyday communication practices (multimodal, multi-authored, digital communication practices, participatory culture—what literacy researchers call "new literacies") that are happening as a result of sophisticated, open access Internet communication technologies (Ito et al., 2010; Jenkins, Ford, & Green, 2013; Lankshear & Knobel, 2010, 2011). This ignoring has made schools dangerously irrelevant to children and youth who are already participating in these practices in authentic (with new ethos) and meaningful ways (Gee, 2004, 2010) and who find school-based practices out of date and inauthentic (old ethos).

Researchers both inside and outside of education have begun to discuss the ways in which traditional institutions such as schools are becoming increasingly irrelevant as formerly passive audiences shift toward a participatory convergence culture outside of formal schooling (Jenkins, 2006). In fields other than education research such as communications and economics, scholars have put forward ideas about the changed nature of society by articulating a focus on what is different in knowledge production now that everyone can participate (Bruns, 2008; Godin, 2008; Jenkins, 2006; Rheingold, 2002; Shirky, 2008, 2010). Wikipedia, open source systems such as Linux, and the mass participation in social networking technologies are consistent with all that educational researchers from a social practice perspective of literacy and learning, for example, have been saying for many years: Learning occurs in meaningful, collaborative participation in culturally valued activities. Whatever we might think of these new practices, whether we think they are beneficial or not, they are the practices we need to account for in schools if we want schools to play a role in knowledge production and meaning making and in shaping our youth.

If we take the example of literacy, we can say that educational researchers have shown that new literacies are predominant in the everyday lives of children and youth yet schools have not figured out how to address these changes, choosing instead to focus on outdated conceptions of literacy as neutral skills separated from their contexts of use and relations of power (Gee, 2004, 2007, 2013a; Janks, 2010; Lankshear & Knobel, 2006, 2010; Leander, 2007). When teachers do use new technologies, they tend to have an "old wine in new bottles" approach that pedagogizes (turns them into traditional "lessons") these robust practices. By not paying attention to the profound level of these changed and changing practices, schools perpetuate and deepen existing gaps in meaning and in equitable access to such practices. Inequitable access is one way that schools are not furthering a justice and equity purpose of schooling.[1]

As I have argued thus far, we know a lot about what should ground the work of schools, yet this work is rarely seen in practice. What might it take to see profound and authentic change that works for a just and equitable system? I argue that we need a new ontological starting point in order to see the change we need. I bring together a diverse set of theoretical principles to describe the mindset that is needed to ground a new system ontologically and epistemologically. My purpose here is to articulate a new ontological position and theoretical foundation upon which a transformed public education could be based. My overall goal in the book is to present a plausible argument for starting over. I do not outline details of what we would need to do as a sort of script, but I discuss principles that need to be in place in order for such a "reboot" to occur.

Specifically, if "we the people" see a role for public schooling in contributing to a just and equitable education system and society, then we need to rethink what is happening in schools. Following Shirky (2010), we need to ask: Do we want to be a part of the conversation our children and youth are already having? To do so, we must recognize a fundamental flaw in education: Schooling is based on the presumption of unequal intelligence. This chapter first describes a different ontological position based on Rancière's work in *The Ignorant Schoolmaster*, and then presents theories that would follow from this new position.

Equality of Intelligence

Schooling is based on an ontological flaw—inequality of intelligence (Rancière, 1991). That is, schooling assumes inequality between humans—those who know and those who do not. Rancière's argument is that we must begin with the assumption of equality of intelligence—all intelligence is equal. All people know. People might know differently, but we all know equally and all these ways of knowing should be valued equally.

To explain what he means, Rancière introduces the idea that instruction assumes that what needs to be learned needs to be explicated, or explained, to someone who does not know. The explicator (the teacher) needs the student (the unintelligent) in order to "instruct." It is thus the explicator, or teacher, who constitutes the student as unintelligent by dividing intelligence in two—one who knows and one who does not. This act results in the child coming to learn that he/she knows nothing without being explained to:

> The child who recites under the threat of the rod obeys the rod and that's all: he will apply his intelligence to something else. But the child who is explained to will devote his intelligence to the work of grieving: to understanding, that is to say, to understanding that he doesn't understand unless he is explained to.
>
> *(Rancière, 1991, p. 8)*

This grieving is what we see today as children and youth increasingly turn their intelligence to things other than school. The enormous rise of fan fiction, anime, and video production among children, youth, and young adults is testimony to this shift in focus (boyd, 2008; Ito et al., 2010; Lammers, 2013). What we need to do is find ways for children and youth to bring their intelligence to school. This is not to say that they should not have multiple outlets for their intelligence, only that school needs to be one of those outlets and currently it is not.

Rancière goes so far as to say that, given an assumption of equality of intelligence, teachers do not have to know the subject matter they are teaching. He claims that the myth of pedagogy is that knowledge needs to be explicated so that the learner can learn. This myth puts the learner in a passive position of receiver of knowledge—much like traditional conceptions in schools where the learner is positioned as an empty head needing to be filled. Rancière argues instead that the pedagogical problem is how to "show intelligence to itself" (1991, p. 28). To do this, one does not have to be expert in whatever content is at play.

The work of showing intelligence to itself is done through a focus on processes of emancipation, not on product (or content). Rancière articulates a process of emancipation that is similar to Freire's (1970) conscientization, or consciousness raising, in that it is about humans working alongside each other to become conscious of their own power and their own knowing. For Rancière, emancipation is a process through which a person comes to see what an "intelligence can do when it considers itself equal to any other and considers any other equal to itself" (1991, p. 39).

I can see the point that teachers do not have to know what they are teaching if all intelligence is equal, but I can also see that this claim could be read as devaluing teachers (in fact, some teachers I work with have said as much when I talked with them about these ideas). I read this protest as a question about how to account for expert content knowledge. However, being expert at something, or being able to teach that knowledge, does not have to position someone else as not knowing, or as unequally intelligent. Rather, depth of content knowledge can lead to maximum pedagogical freedom in that expert and novice can come together to show intelligence to itself in exciting and authentic ways. A problem-posing pedagogy (Freire, 1970), such as I describe below in the Lunch Is Gross project example, provides all learners with the opportunity to contribute equally to ongoing activity.

To understand equality of contribution, we need a theory that helps us account for equal contribution and expert content knowledge. Using the principles of equipotentiality, or that each person can contribute something valuable to ongoing activity, teachers' (as learners) content knowledge is what they contribute. Students (as learners) will have their own contribution. Together they will build new knowledge instead of regurgitating old and outdated knowledge. Together, teachers as students and students as teachers (Freire, 1970) build new knowledge as they seek to find answers to the presented problem. Everyone is a learner focused on problem solving rather than being divided into those who know and those who do not. Historical knowledge (what we already know in the disciplines) would come to bear on the problem under examination as both teachers and students bring their knowledge to the activity.

A personal example might help readers understand what it means to consider all intelligence as equal. I belong to a knitting group where all levels of knitting ability are included without judgment in the activity of gathering to knit. We have expert knitters who have been knitting for over 30 years, young people who are just getting started, and younger and older people who are experts. Others, like me, are at an intermediate level. We gather twice a week to knit and talk about any and all topics; nothing is off limits. All intelligence is equal, even though abilities vary. That I am an intermediate knitter does not compromise my ability to participate in the group; I count—everybody does, expert and novice. Our goal (problem), even with different knitting projects, is to knit. We help each other without formal "instruction" by knitting together and talking about our projects. In this way, we all contribute to intelligence seeing itself.

Rancière is arguing against the need for instruction and against the need for the teacher to know what they are teaching about. He uses the example of his main character Jocotot's experience teaching literature in a country in which he did not speak the language of his students. Furthermore, the book was not in the students' language. Jocotot simply gave the students the book and told them to come back when they had figured it out. To his surprise, they did. From this experience, he realized the intelligence of his students as they came to see intelligence themselves.

How would this play out in contemporary times? This is definitely not the Middle Ages as in Rancière's story of Jocotot. I argue that if we bring in the concept of equipotentiality, we can account for all participants in the learning activity being able to know something and that all of those "somethings" can be brought to bear on the activity itself. I have already talked about linking this to Freire's problem-posing curriculum, but being dependent on some kind of "problem" may not be sustainable. Plus, there are things that contemporary society has agreed we want our children to know. How will we account for this content? When I discuss equipotential participation below, I show how content might come to bear on intelligence seeing itself.

Before moving to discuss the theories that would follow from this new ontological position I need to say that by equality of intelligence *I do not mean sameness.* Perhaps it would be more appropriate to use the term equity of intelligence to account for the complete uniqueness of each individual intelligence and way of learning. Equipotentiality, or the equal potential to contribute (see next section), helps account for these variances given the main principle that everyone has equal opportunity (again, not the same opportunity) to contribute something meaningful to the learning process. Equity of intelligence requires that each way of showing intelligence to itself would be different and that difference would be valued. Every person, however, has the right to be included in this process; everybody means everybody and everybody counts. We need a way to account for how everyone can participate knowing that everyone is different. Equipotentiality provides a framework for understanding this.

What if, instead, we assumed equality of intelligence between all participants in the schooling endeavor? What would follow from this ontological change? Equality is a practice, not a state. That we need to practice equality on a daily basis is a profound restatement or re-envisioning of the starting point we need in education. We need to begin by assuming equality of intelligence. When we do this, education becomes showing intelligence to itself rather than a process of explication.

With the ontological shift to equality of intelligence, we need different theories of participation, knowledge production, and collaboration. I discuss some suggestions next.

Equipotentiality

We need a theory of equal participation that accounts for all intelligence being equal, including teacher (or other expert) content knowledge. Equipotentiality assumes that, while the skills and abilities of all participants in the produsage project are not the same, they all have an equal ability to make a worthy contribution (Bruns, 2008). Consistent with Rancière's concept that all intelligence is equal, equipotentiality accounts for differential content knowledge and ability. A key contribution of equipotentiality is that *all* participants have the ability to contribute to ongoing activity—no exceptions—everybody means everybody. When I speak to teachers and colleagues about this idea, people almost always bring up "what if" questions, with people with intellectual disabilities such as Down syndrome as examples of someone whose intelligence is not equal. I argue that their intelligence is equal, just different. Someone with Down syndrome can equipotentially participate in a learning activity by contributing in a way they are capable (Burrello, Sailor, & Kleinhammer-Tramill, 2013; Nussbaum, 2011). That one way may be key to the success of the activity itself. All intelligence is equally valuable, but that does not mean all intelligence is the same.

Teaching and learning happen when people participate together in goal directed activities and practices (Cole, 1996; Gutierrez & Rogoff, 2003; Rogoff, 2003, 2011). Given the equipotential nature of participation in these activities, how participation is structured changes. In equipotential participation structures, participation roles position everyone as a teacher and everyone as a learner in activities in which power relations are heterarchical, or in which what Kress (2010) calls horizontal participation is possible. In contrast to traditional hierarchical participation, in *heterarchical participation structures,* there is open participation and communal evaluation as people participate fluidly and equipotentially in ongoing activities and practices. Participation is always fluid. Heterarchical participation limits the ability of one person to exclusively dictate the content and direction of activity while decisions, including decisions about what content should be considered,[2] are made ad hoc and in the moment. These activities are not without power relations, but these relations are not structurally permanent and remain constantly in flux. While leadership and power are not always the same thing, the point is that both are fluid and everyone can occupy the spaces for leadership and power. How knowledge gets constructed when there is equal participation can be accommodated for in a theory of knowledge production that accounts for everyone participating with equal intelligence. Bruns' concept of produsage accomplishes this accounting.

Produsage

Bruns (2008) introduces the concept of produsage to explain the new forms of knowledge production associated with the advent of Internet communication technologies (ICT). Produsage means that we use the knowledge we produce in a collaborative process of user-led knowledge production that bypasses

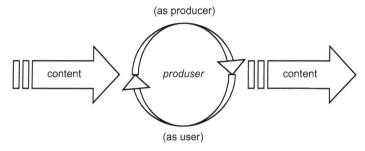

FIGURE 2.1 Produsage model
Source: Bruns, 2008. http://produsage.org/node/9

traditional hierarchical, expert-driven models of knowledge production and distribution common in U.S. schooling. It is the "collaborative and continuous building and extending of existing content in pursuit of further improvement" (Bruns, 2008, p. 21) that guides the knowledge produsage process. "We the people" have shifted from a consumer model to a produsage model in ways that go beyond simply a producer (de Certeau, 1984) to a hybrid produser (producer/user) (see Figure 2.1). The knowledge-producing school model discussed in Chapter 5 is one way to implement this principle.

Produsage assumes that knowledge is always in the process of development, and that information and knowledge are unfinished, extensible, and evolving intercreatively through the collaborative production of shared informational resources of common interest, rather than receiving already existing knowledge and information (Bruns, 2008). Given the principle of equipotentiality that everyone[3] has the potential to make a valuable contribution (heterarchical participation), there is no need for prior formal filtering for participation because evaluation happens in use. This facilitates the capillary circulation of power (Foucault, 1978) in heterarchical relationships, as opposed to the hierarchal model of experts dictating actions. Power is circulated vertically and horizontally in the produsage model.

My knitting group provides some insight into what this might look like. As I mentioned, a group of knitters meets weekly at a local yarn shop to knit and talk together with the main purpose being to knit. Knowledge about knitting in general and individual projects in particular are prodused as people participate in the activity of knitting. Evaluation is done fluidly and non-judgmentally through interaction while knitting. No one person directs the activity; however, expert knowledge is still evident and brought to bear when needed. There is no end point to what can be known or learned about knitting that someone will then evaluate as "good." As one member often states, "There are no knitting police." What is possible to know about knitting is ever growing and evolving through the produsage of knitting itself. School content (literacy, math, science, social studies, language) could be learned in similar ways.

Given the equality of intelligence and the knowledge produsage process, we also need a theory of collaboration that can help us understand how people participate together to produse knowledge in new times.

Mass Collaboration

In his discussion of what is changing with advanced communication technologies, Shirky (2008) asks what changes when everybody comes as a way to introduce concepts associated with mass collaboration. He argues that we are in the middle of a profound revolution in human communication and organization that parallels the changes that occurred with the invention of the printing press that gave everyone access to readership. "We the people," formerly known as the audience, can now communicate, organize, and advocate without formal organizations or corporations to tell us how. We have access to authorship as we shift from one-to-many to many-to-many communication structures similar to heterarchical structures discussed in the previous section (Shirky, 2008). The printing press gave us access to text; the Internet gives us access to authorship (developed by participating in the act of authoring) and to social action in unprecedented ways (Rheingold, 2002), hence the profound nature of the changes.

With these changes in communication and organization has come a shift in role from audience/consumer to producer (or what Bruns would call produser) of multiple forms of knowledge. As Shirky (2010) explains, there are a trillion hours of leisure time available to us that, when television was the main source of entertainment, we turned over to watching and consuming as a passive audience. With advanced Internet and communication technologies, we have shifted our focus and redirected what Shirky calls a cognitive surplus to creative social endeavors that bring together digital technology, human generosity, and our profound desire to share. Not all of these new uses of time are world changing—we do have LOL (laugh out loud) cats, as Shirky points out. But we also have significant spaces where huge numbers of people can get and produse knowledge and information and use that information for civic purposes (Rheingold, 2002). Shirky gives the example of OryEcola and the development of the Ushahidi website (www.ushahidi.com/) to explain this more civic-minded use. Ecola's blog, "Kenyan Pundit," published information about violence occurring in East Africa but was soon overwhelmed by people sending notices. Two programmers took 72 hours to develop the Ushahidi website, which took this information, aggregated it, and made it available worldwide. They then made the site open source, thus available to everyone to use and adapt. The speed with which this knowledge was produced and disseminated is a clear example of how profoundly communication has changed.

The challenge Shirky poses is to first understand the difference between communal value of these activities (LOL cats or some affinity spaces like my knitting group) and civic value (Ushahidi). What I suggest is that as educators we already tend toward the civic value of our actions so, given these new

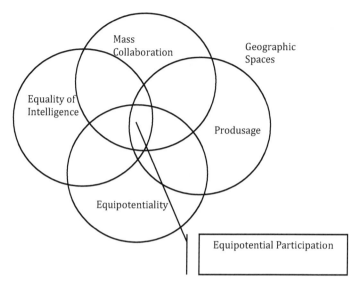

FIGURE 2.2 Equipotential participation

opportunities, we do not have to wait for NCLB and RTTT to be changed (or to wait for Superman). We can organize ourselves to make the changes we know are needed. We are millions of mouths who can now talk back in ways that were not possible before. Some of these actions have begun with such movements as Save Our Schools (http://saveourschoolsmarch.org Retrieved 10/27/12) and anti-testing movements (http://unitedoptout.com Retrieved 10/27/12). More are needed in order to achieve the changes we need as we start over.

By bringing these concepts together, we can build a new ontological and epistemological foundation upon which to ground starting over in U.S. education. With all intelligence as equal, we can construct contexts for learning in which all participants can equipotentially contribute to the knowledge produsage project. Schools can play a vital role in the construction of such spaces rather than constraining them. We can see the space of overlap into which we might place this type of learning in schools (see Figure 2.2). In this model, all participants are of equal intelligence, all participants' knowledge and cultural practices count in the ongoing construction of new knowledge, and all participants have equal potential to contribute. All of this occurs in specific geographies, which warrants additional attention to space and spatial theories.

Spatial Justice

Given that knowledge production and meaning making occur in specific geographies, it is important to bring in the concept of space and spatial justice to understand how space shapes and is shaped by these processes. In Figure 2.2, space is all the white space; it is physical, social, and virtual. Theories of critical geography complement the theoretical perspective I have described thus far by identifying the consequences of space on sociality, including, I would argue, digital spaces—a key component of authentic learning (e.g., learning something new rather than regurgitating what is already known). Soja (2003) argues that "spatiality is socially produced and, like society itself, exists in both substantial forms (concrete spatialities) and as a set of relations between individuals and groups, an 'embodiment' and medium of social life itself" (p. 120). In this view, spatial structures are historically and materially constituted in the social relations that evolve over time. My knitting group, for example, happens in a particular knitting shop in Rochester, New York. There are two other such shops, each with its own knitting group and each with its own unique culture (although there would be some similarities given the culture of knitters as a whole; cf. Gutiérrez & Rogoff, 2003). The variations between shops in geographic location matter in terms of what and how knowledge is prodused and what social relations are constructed. Each shop is located in different suburbs and thus has differently classed patrons, for example.

Soja (2010) argues that social science researchers have privileged the social and historical when studying human practices to the exclusion of spatial practices and that this exclusion has allowed spatial injustices to fester, such as access to food as in the Freedom Market example that follows. He challenges us to include the spatial in a tripartite ontological analysis (social, historical, and spatial) in order to more fully understand human meaning making. Human actions literally take place; they occur in places and spaces. Our actions tend to focus on particular centers and this centering generates unevenly distributed advantages and disadvantages, depending on location and accessibility with respect to the center. The example of the Freedom Market that I will discuss shortly is connected to the concept of fighting for the right to the city and illustrates how centering can result in spatial injustices.

What does it mean to fight for the right to the city? The meaning is in the term itself—that people have the right to the geographies in which they live. Lefebvre (1991) argues that the everyday workings of life in the city generate unequal power relationships, which produce inequitable and unjust distributions of social resources, such as grocery stores, across the space of the city. Seeking the right to the city is a continual process of claiming (and reclaiming) an active presence. I use the case of the Freedom Market as an example of the potential of urban residents working for their right to the city that takes as starting points equipotential participation, knowledge produsage, and mass collaboration. Transforming the corner store is an activity in which the "everybody" of this neighborhood community equipotentially participates in a knowledge produsage project.

In the following section, I will ground the ideas discussed so far in two examples: one in an urban elementary school classroom where students protested the bad lunch food through the production of a documentary film (Gatto, 2012b, 2013) and one in which residents are in the process of changing their neighborhood in positive ways through the establishment of the Freedom Market (Larson & Moses, 2012; Larson et al., 2013). Both examples show how these concepts work together; however, each is presented with particular principles in mind. The student-produced documentary is one example of what equipotentiality and produsage look like in an urban elementary classroom. The Freedom Market example shows what mass collaboration and fighting for the right to the city look like in a community setting.

Lunch Is Gross

In the first example, one exemplary veteran urban elementary teacher, Lynn Gatto,[4] and her students became increasingly frustrated with what they perceived were disgusting school lunches. The lunches had become something of a joke. However, given that 89% of the students in this class received free and reduced lunches[5] and relied on this food as a key source of their daily nutrition, the situation was not funny (Gatto, 2013). The class wondered how their lunches came about and whether they could get them changed. What resulted was a complex unit of study in which students investigated the "relationship between power and language by asking complex questions about race relations, resource inequities, and institutional politics, and then designing a new text in order to change their social future" (Gatto, 2013, p. 242).

To have a clearer picture of the value of this Lunch Is Gross project, it is important to know that the 22 mostly African American and Latino students in Gatto's class lived in the poorest achieving school district in New York State in a city with the seventh highest child poverty rate in the U.S. (Spector, 2012). No joke indeed. She had several students with Individual Education Programs,[6] or IEPs, as well.

Gatto had been eating lunch with her students and came to see that the majority of them threw out their lunches, going hungry rather than eating them. She and her students realized something had to be done. After a lively class discussion, the class decided to do research on nutrition and how they might take action to get healthier lunches. They conducted interviews, gave surveys to kids, parents, and school staff, and did newspaper research to find out what variations occurred across urban and suburban districts. Students were outraged to see the differences in food selection between their district and local suburban school district offerings. In partnership with a local corporation and news station, they produced a documentary based on their research (Gatto, 2012b).

The idea for the film project came entirely from the students. As was a common part of her classroom practice, Gatto facilitated the process and contributed her expertise where relevant and needed (Larson & Marsh, 2005). Gatto based her practice on a critical literacy framework and social practice view of learning

(Gatto, 2013). The collaboration with a local news station enabled the students to have a professional news set within which to stage their broadcast. When students attempted to show the film at a school board meeting and were denied, Gatto and students then posted it to Teacher Tube. They wrote an email to the school board and the superintendent letting them know they had done so. The superintendent contacted Gatto within 20 minutes of receiving the email saying he would come to see the lunches for himself (Gatto, 2013). He, too, was disgusted and promised to make significant changes. Gatto and the students continued their advocacy work even though school was over and onto the next year. After having garnered news coverage, Gatto and her students were given a grant from a local health foundation to continue their work. They organized a march at school district offices where a large group of people showed up. They picketed with signs that resulted in more press coverage (see Figure 2.3). In the end, the district changed its food provider, at least partly as a result of the students' work.

Content learning came to bear on the activity in several ways. The literacy practices in which students in this example participated were rich and engaging, varying from writing letters (including to the editor of the local newspaper) to using teleprompters to write the scripts they read while filming (Gatto, 2013). Math practices were needed to analyze surveys and to display the findings. Science learning occurred as they researched what counted as nutrition. And social studies were used to understand urban/suburban differences. Furthermore, they engaged in critical social action through their picketing at which they were interviewed by the media, and then spoke to a standing-room-only crowd at a school board meeting.

FIGURE 2.3 Students picketing the school district central office
Source: Photo by Rachel Pickering.

In this example, we can see what the principles I have articulated look like in an urban classroom. All intelligence was equally valued in the conception and production of the film, including the teacher, and no one person was in control of the content or the process. Individuals contributed according to their own interest and ability. Each student and Gatto had potential and opportunity to equipotentially participate in the project. Evaluation was fluid and occurred in the flow of interaction during production, and high standards were held. Decisions about content and process were made ad hoc and in the moment over the course of the production of the film. This is not to say they did not carefully plan the film, construct storyboards, do substantial research on healthy foods and suburban lunch menus, and other practices needed to produce a high quality product. Knowledge produsage was rigorous and meaningful, especially as the end result was a change in the district's food vendor. Spatial boundaries blurred as students moved easily across spaces for learning (school, community, business) to produse the film, thus dismantling the in/out of school binary.

Although I am making an argument to start over in education, it is important to acknowledge that there are many teachers who exemplify the principles I have shared. I am not suggesting we ignore their work. Rather, we need to find these teachers and follow their lead. Lynn Gatto was such a teacher. She was an award-winning teacher but one who bucked the system at every point. She always did what she considered right for kids and got national teaching awards, but was unpopular among peers, who often acted against her publicly and privately. She was proud of her letters of insubordination. Most of what she did would not be possible today under current standards and accountability mandates. There are teachers like Gatto all across the country. We need to trust these teachers to be the professionals they are and treat them accordingly.

Freedom Market Project

The Freedom Market[7] project is a powerful example of one community's attempt to take back the city, one that embodies the kind of collaborative work needed in contemporary society. The project was started by a local community organization, Northeast Area Development (NEAD). NEAD is a community development organization whose purpose is to improve the surrounding neighborhood through real estate development, community organizing, and educational activism. It uses a cultural framework based in the seven principles of Kwanzaa, or *nguzo saba* (unity, self-determination, collective work and responsibility, cooperative economics, purpose, creativity, and faith), as an orienting and guiding set of principles in their work (cf. www.officialkwanzaawebsite. org/NguzoSaba.shtml for further information). NEAD hosts a local Children's Defense Fund Freedom School that also follows these principles, which serves area children and youth after school and during the summer. In collaboration with community residents, we are doing participatory action research (McIntyre,

2008) on the Freedom Market project (see Figure 2.4), with supportive funding from a local health foundation.

The Freedom Market is located across the street from NEAD's main offices. The neighborhood has approximately 5,900 residents who are majority African American and Latino. Area challenges include: (1) absentee landlords whose properties are of substandard quality; (2) deteriorated and deteriorating buildings; and (3) a significant number of City-owned vacant properties. While there are challenges, the neighborhood works hard to build on its assets such as: (1) involved

FIGURE 2.4 Freedom Market
Source: Photo by Joanne Larson.

neighborhood residents; (2) a strong sense of cultural unity; and (3) a comprehensive development organization (NEAD).

With no supermarkets within the neighborhood itself, the residents do not have ready access to affordable, fresh, and healthy food; they live in what has been called an urban "food desert" (Pothukuchi, 2005; USDA, 2013). McClintock (2011) suggests that food deserts disproportionately impact people from nondominant groups and lower-income neighborhoods and communities, where in many of these urban spaces there exists uneven community development and imbalanced relationships of power. Food deserts are one example of spatial injustice that arises when the "centering" that Lefebvre (1991) discusses occurs. However, we find that people in this community live in a food swamp (The Week, 2013). In other words, they are inundated with unhealthy food, rather than having nearby access to clean, healthy foods. There is a public market in an adjacent neighborhood, but it is not open every day and residents report that the market is for "tourists."

Because the area is extremely low-income (median income less than $20,000 per year, U.S. Census, 2010), many residents do not have cars and must rely on public transportation to get to the places they need to go. While public transportation is an option for cheap and efficient mobility, it is not conducive to carrying several days' worth of groceries. One can only take a few grocery bags on a crowded city bus at any given time, forcing residents to select light, portable goods over heavier, cumbersome products (such as fruit and vegetables). To get to a full-service supermarket, residents need to take a taxi. At approximately $10–15 per round-trip, this takes a sizeable chunk of the household grocery budget, an option many households in the neighborhood do not have. However, they can walk to ubiquitous corner stores as they walk "their" city (de Certeau, 1984).

This economic condition has resulted in the only alternative for these families being grocery shopping at high-priced corner stores, largely stocked with high-fat, packaged foods that provide little to no nutritional value. There are 94 such markets in the northeast of Rochester alone (where the market is located). The Freedom Market project is revamping a current corner store to introduce a larger variety of healthy food options to residents. By transforming the corner store, we offer the neighborhood an alternative that will phase in healthier and more affordable food options over a 3-year period.

Soja (2010, p. 99) claims that urban residents have the following spatial rights: (1) to participate openly and fairly in all processes producing urban space; (2) to access and make use of particular advantages of urban life; (3) to avoid all forms of imposed spatial segregation and confinement; and (4) to be provided with public services that meet basic needs in health, education, and welfare. The Freedom Market project is attempting to facilitate these rights, specifically those relating to meeting basic needs in health.

Observations at the market have shown that some residents, children and adults, come into the store eight to ten times daily. Sometimes they purchase snacks, sometimes lottery tickets, and sometimes just to chat. When interviewed, they talk about not having family dinners and eating mostly fast food. The corner store is a physical and geographic space where the neighborhood comes for snack foods, soda, beer, and tobacco products, and to build and sustain social relationships. Importantly, the social connection and community "check in" seems to be a key to the role of the store as a convergence space of comfort and safety; it feels like "home." Some of the market's staff have insisted on transcending the pejorative conception of corner store in favor of the corner store as *cornerstone* of the community (much like churches have historically represented a social and political center in the African American community). In this way, the market not only provides physical nourishment, but also educational, emotional, and spiritual sustenance. Moreover, NEAD's purpose in taking over the store is to take back the neighborhood marketplace as a gathering space for healthy interaction and healthy food.

A key feature of the research we have been doing together has been what participants refer to as "community defined evidence"; in other words, they are the experts on themselves and they do not need outside "researchers" telling them who they are or what they need to do. In other words, their intelligence is equal and should be valued. They define their evidence by community discussion over time, one way everyone participates. In this way, they are taking back research—who defines them and who decides what they need—in much the same way as they are taking back the city. This view values local knowledge in culturally relevant ways:

> A range of treatment approaches and supports that are derived from, and supportive of, the positive cultural attributes of the local society and traditions, Practice Based Evidence (what this project calls Community Defined Evidence) services are accepted as effective by the local community, through community consensus, and address the therapeutic and healing needs of individuals and families from a culturally-specific framework. Practitioners of practice based evidence models draw upon cultural knowledge and traditions for treatments and are respectfully responsive to the local definitions of wellness and dysfunction.
>
> *(Isaacs, Huang, Hernandez, & Echo-Hawk, 2005, n.p.)*

Community defined evidence takes into consideration a person's worldview, the collective thought process of a people or culture, the social and historical context, as well as communication styles, which are all culturally rooted. In other words, all intelligence is equal and all participation counts. Consequently, in the Freedom Market project participants have developed surveys for store customers and an observational notes sheet for "food corps" workers to use while working in the store. A key part of the store is that it is a research space where workers do not just wait for the cash register transaction, but work for transformative interactions as co-researchers. The store represents multiple spaces for residents in what Foucault calls a heterotopia.

Store as Heterotopia

Foucault (1967, p. 5) provided a provocative way of thinking about the spatial intersections of cultural production, place, and history such as we see in the store. The heterotopia, he suggested, is a place that is "at once mythic and real," that takes on changeable meanings which are culturally specific but also fluid, and is "capable of juxtaposing in a single real place several spaces that are in themselves incompatible." A theory of heterotopic spaces, in other words, can handle simultaneous contradictions, and sees these as inevitable and universal. Western scientific modes of thinking are obligated to "resolve" such contradictions and determine what and where a place is—collapsing possibilities into recognizable models. But thinking through heterotopia and convergence, what seem to be incompatibilities or differences (such as continuing to sell alcohol and lottery tickets) can be reframed as generative tensions that fuel interactions and instigate change—new ways of thinking and being. I suggest that such new ways of thinking and being are needed to start over in education.

The store itself is a space of convergence, convergence of bodies in one space with multiple goals—not just food sales (see Figure 2.5). The center of the figure is where the store does its work: a geographic convergence of multiple spaces through which community residents take back their rights to the city. Our analysis has shown that social spaces with local cultural practices around food and other practices are of primary importance to residents as they patronize the store. The

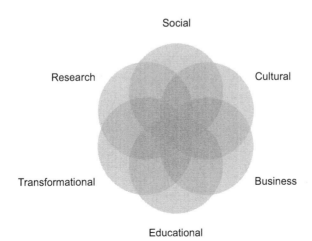

FIGURE 2.5 Spatial convergences

store is a business, so business practices pervade what is a business space. As co-researchers, co-authors, and co-implementers, we all participate in constructing the store as a research space through which transformation in the community occurs. As we have learned about various math and literacy practices of residents, the store is an educational space as we work with customers to build upon some of these practices.

In this convergence heterotopia, assumptions of dualities between consumer/producer and buyer/seller are reconfigured. Store workers are positioned to "serve" patrons, but this service is an interactive and reciprocal process of building a restorative culture and of researching that culture, not simply maximizing profits. Kids entering before 2 p.m. on weekdays are expected to answer for why they are not at school. Children bring their homework to share with store workers, sometimes receiving help to finish it. When patrons select unhealthy snack options, they are gently reminded of fresh fruit options available on the shelf just behind them, or when they select healthy options, they are given praise and "high fives." Counter persons get to know patrons' names and their family's names, their likes and dislikes, and what they would like to see at the store. What might seem like savvy marketing research is authentic culture building. It is care.

The market exemplifies how mass collaboration and knowledge produsage come together to produce authentic change. While the change is slow, there is evidence that store customers, through trusting relationships, are changing how they eat and how they think about health. We have seen a dramatic increase in the purchase of water instead of sugary drinks, for example. Knowledge is prodused collaboratively through the participatory action research and through interactions in the store as we share our findings with customers.

Both of these examples offer new ways of constructing spaces for learning in schools and elsewhere. We can account for equality of intelligence like Gatto and her students by valuing all knowledge in the production of a jointly designed project. We can construct learning spaces as heterotopias, as NEAD has done with the Freedom Market. By developing community defined evidence as co-researchers, NEAD has constructed a space that understands and fully incorporates community values. They have changed the space in order to accommodate the multiple spaces of the community and to foster changed relationships. In both cases, participants were able to re-imagine their future in ways not possible in traditional settings. In these ways and others that use the principles outlined here, "we the people" can take back education.

Guiding Principles

To sum up, I articulate a set of principles as guides to the work of starting over:

1. *All intelligence is equal.* While all intelligence is not the same, everyone knows and can produse knowledge in collaboration with others. Following this principle, pedagogy becomes showing intelligence to itself.

2.   *All participants have equal opportunity to cont*
     knowledge produsage process. Since all intellige
     be afforded the possibility of contributing to
     Accommodations should be made for peopl
     linguistic differences so their participation is
     edge produsage process.

3.   *Participation is based on shared interest (affinit*
     ticipation based on interest rather than a pr
     markers based on race, class, gender, ability, language .
     away. Participation is defined by other means (e.g., expertise).

4.   *Knowledge is prodused (not simply retained or replicated) in interaction for real audi-*
     ences and purposes. Following the principles of knowledge produsage as using
     what we produce, knowledge production moves beyond the simple replica-
     tion of existing knowledge to the authentic produsage of knowledge that is
     immediately used by real audiences for real purposes. Knowledge is thus fluid
     and constantly in production rather than existing as a static body outside of
     human interaction that can be memorized and tested.

5.   *Meaningful learning is relevant to all participants and to their everyday lives and occurs*
     beyond the confines of material space. Given that participation in the knowledge
     produsage process is interest based, relevance to participants is a key aspect
     of meaning making. That real audiences can immediately use knowledge for
     real purposes makes the learning process meaningful and ubiquitous. Tradi-
     tional boundaries of the school building as the only site of "real" learning
     disappear.

6.   *Form and content of knowledge produsage are in dialectic relation, always changing,*
     and fluid. By dialectic, I mean that form and content are mutually constituted.
     In other words, form shapes content and content shapes form, thus ensuring
     fluidity and avoiding static fixations of "bits" of knowledge as often happens
     in traditional models.

7.   *Social action is paired with ease of participation to produse change.* Mass collabora-
     tion afforded by Internet communication technologies enables social action
     to take place on larger scales. Change is possible in unprecedented ways now
     that everyone can come and everyone counts.

8.   *Space is socially produced and materially grounded.* Space, including spaces for
     learning, is produced interactionally as humans produse knowledge. This
     affords fluidity in where learning can happen in ways that avoid the in/out of
     school binary.

9.   *Social relationships are of primary importance.* Humans build relationships. We
     must build trusting relationships with children and youth as one way to come
     to know the diverse range of funds of knowledge available.

I suggest a reconceptualization of contexts for learning that focus more on
collaborative heterarchical participation in authentic, purposeful activity than on
memorizing or testing decontextualized skills or bounding learning in specific

, and hope that merging these scholarly frames will help us potentially the casual collapse of education.

tice and equity in schools needs to include heterarchical power relations, uipotential participation structures, and the right to meaningful (inclusive) spaces. The change needed is not about bringing outside practices "in" and pedagogizing them, but it is about using the interpretation of the principles of learning and goals of practice this book offers to construct curricula that embody those principles and practices in the context of authentic and expansive learning. We might connect these principles to Freire's notion of problem-posing and generative theme curriculum, or to Bigum's (2002) idea of knowledge-producing schools as a possible structure around which we could develop curricula alongside children and youth (and communities) in ways that would align with the new purpose of schooling articulated in Chapter 3.

What would this look like? We would see community members of all ages alongside children and youth in collaboratively organized, joint participation in goal-directed, interest-driven activity working to solve real world problems with real world audiences, such as those described in the examples given in this chapter. The focus would be on the process of learning not on a fixed product, like a high-stakes test. The learning space would be a safe space, a heterotopia, for experimentation and error that allows for innovation. Power would be heterarchically organized in ways that account for multiple forms of participation. Equipotential participation would be open to everyone and everyone would count. The emphasis would be on building social relationships while working for social and spatial justice in real world activity. The purposes of the activity would be shared and collaboratively constructed with social justice goals.

Some readers might suggest that many of these principles have been articulated previously in educational literature. I agree. I have referred to some of this literature in Table 2.1 below and throughout the book. Furthermore, I have put the educational work alongside the theories I present in this chapter so that parallels can be more easily seen.

It is important that we see the parallels across these literatures and not act as though conversations have not begun. They have begun. But so far, intellectual conversation has not been enough to affect the kind of change we need to respond to current changes in communication and collaboration, or to build a just and equitable system. What concerns me is that in spite of the rigor and authenticity in the educational literature cited here, schools remain unjust and inequitable spaces for children and youth. As I have suggested, this is unacceptable and can no longer be allowed. Someone has to say, "enough!" This book is my attempt at such an exclamation.

This chapter has articulated new ontological and epistemological underpinnings to starting over in education. While we need these new foundations, we cannot maintain the traditional worker/citizen binary purpose of school and expect change. I turn to articulating a possible new purpose in the next chapter.

TABLE 2.1 Connecting Theoretical Frameworks

Theory	Related educational theory
Equipotentiality: • All participants have an equal opportunity to contribute something valuable to the learning activity.	Community of learners (Rogoff, 1994). Vertical and horizontal participation (Gutiérrez, 2008; Kress, 2010). Funds of knowledge (Moll et al., 1992). Culturally relevant pedagogy (Gay, 2010; Ladson-Billings, 1995). Affinity spaces (Gee, 2004). Engaged pedagogy (hooks, 1994).
Produsage: • We use the knowledge we produce in a collaborative process of user-led knowledge production.	Knowledge as socially constructed (Berger & Luckmann, 1967). Community of learners (Rogoff, 1994). Communities of practice (Lave & Wenger, 1991).
Mass collaboration: • People can now communicate, organize, and advocate without formal organizations. • Shift from one-to-many to many-to-many communication structures.	Sociocultural learning theories (Cole, 1996; Gutiérrez & Rogoff, 2003; Moll, 1990; Vygotsky, 1978, 1986). Participation structures (Goffman, 1981; Larson, 1995).
Spatial justice: • Spatial structures are historically and materially constituted in the social relations that evolve over time. • Include the spatial in a tripartite analysis (social, historical, and spatial).	Spatial theories in education (Kinloch, 2010; Leander & Sheahy, 2004).

Notes

1 I have articulated other ways in which schools perpetuate inequities along identity marker lines such as race, class, gender, sexual orientation, language, and ability, in Chapter 1.

2 That content is decided in the moment by the group does not take away the ability of the teacher to draw on her/his own content knowledge to guide decisions or to bring what we already know about a subject to bear on the problem/issue at hand. Here would be a place where we can account for the knowledge that society wants new generations to know, and for disciplinary content knowledge.

3 This assumes that all people have equal access to communication in multiple forms. In other words, that accommodations for people with disability labels and with linguistic differences are in place so that equipotential participation is a genuine reality.

4 The Lunch Is Gross example is taken from Gatto's (2012a) dissertation.

5 A proxy for poverty level.
6 Law in the U.S. requires IEPs for students with disability labels. They outline learning goals and objectives as well as accommodations tailored for the student.
7 The following section is adapted from: Larson, J., Hanny, C., Moses, G., and Boatwright, T. (2012, April). Spaces of geographic convergence culture. Paper presented at the annual meeting of the American Educational Research Association, Vancouver, British Columbia.

2. *All participants have equal opportunity to contribute something valuable to the knowledge produsage process.* Since all intelligence is equal, everyone should be afforded the possibility of contributing to ongoing knowledge produsage. Accommodations should be made for people with disability labels and with linguistic differences so their participation is an authentic part of the knowledge produsage process.

3. *Participation is based on shared interest (affinity), not identity markers.* With participation based on interest rather than a priori curricula, traditional identity markers based on race, class, gender, ability, language, or sexual orientation fall away. Participation is defined by other means (e.g., expertise).

4. *Knowledge is prodused (not simply retained or replicated) in interaction for real audiences and purposes.* Following the principles of knowledge produsage as using what we produce, knowledge production moves beyond the simple replication of existing knowledge to the authentic produsage of knowledge that is immediately used by real audiences for real purposes. Knowledge is thus fluid and constantly in production rather than existing as a static body outside of human interaction that can be memorized and tested.

5. *Meaningful learning is relevant to all participants and to their everyday lives and occurs beyond the confines of material space.* Given that participation in the knowledge produsage process is interest based, relevance to participants is a key aspect of meaning making. That real audiences can immediately use knowledge for real purposes makes the learning process meaningful and ubiquitous. Traditional boundaries of the school building as the only site of "real" learning disappear.

6. *Form and content of knowledge produsage are in dialectic relation, always changing, and fluid.* By dialectic, I mean that form and content are mutually constituted. In other words, form shapes content and content shapes form, thus ensuring fluidity and avoiding static fixations of "bits" of knowledge as often happens in traditional models.

7. *Social action is paired with ease of participation to produse change.* Mass collaboration afforded by Internet communication technologies enables social action to take place on larger scales. Change is possible in unprecedented ways now that everyone can come and everyone counts.

8. *Space is socially produced and materially grounded.* Space, including spaces for learning, is produced interactionally as humans produse knowledge. This affords fluidity in where learning can happen in ways that avoid the in/out of school binary.

9. *Social relationships are of primary importance.* Humans build relationships. We must build trusting relationships with children and youth as one way to come to know the diverse range of funds of knowledge available.

I suggest a reconceptualization of contexts for learning that focus more on collaborative heterarchical participation in authentic, purposeful activity than on memorizing or testing decontextualized skills or bounding learning in specific geographies, and hope that merging these scholarly frames will help us potentially stem off the casual collapse of education.

Justice and equity in schools needs to include heterarchical power relations, equipotential participation structures, and the right to meaningful (inclusive) spaces. The change needed is not about bringing outside practices "in" and pedagogizing them, but it is about using the interpretation of the principles of learning and goals of practice this book offers to construct curricula that embody those principles and practices in the context of authentic and expansive learning. We might connect these principles to Freire's notion of problem-posing and generative theme curriculum, or to Bigum's (2002) idea of knowledge-producing schools as a possible structure around which we could develop curricula alongside children and youth (and communities) in ways that would align with the new purpose of schooling articulated in Chapter 3.

What would this look like? We would see community members of all ages alongside children and youth in collaboratively organized, joint participation in goal-directed, interest-driven activity working to solve real world problems with real world audiences, such as those described in the examples given in this chapter. The focus would be on the process of learning not on a fixed product, like a high-stakes test. The learning space would be a safe space, a heterotopia, for experimentation and error that allows for innovation. Power would be heterarchically organized in ways that account for multiple forms of participation. Equipotential participation would be open to everyone and everyone would count. The emphasis would be on building social relationships while working for social and spatial justice in real world activity. The purposes of the activity would be shared and collaboratively constructed with social justice goals.

Some readers might suggest that many of these principles have been articulated previously in educational literature. I agree. I have referred to some of this literature in Table 2.1 below and throughout the book. Furthermore, I have put the educational work alongside the theories I present in this chapter so that parallels can be more easily seen.

It is important that we see the parallels across these literatures and not act as though conversations have not begun. They have begun. But so far, intellectual conversation has not been enough to affect the kind of change we need to respond to current changes in communication and collaboration, or to build a just and equitable system. What concerns me is that in spite of the rigor and authenticity in the educational literature cited here, schools remain unjust and inequitable spaces for children and youth. As I have suggested, this is unacceptable and can no longer be allowed. Someone has to say, "enough!" This book is my attempt at such an exclamation.

This chapter has articulated new ontological and epistemological underpinnings to starting over in education. While we need these new foundations, we cannot maintain the traditional worker/citizen binary purpose of school and expect change. I turn to articulating a possible new purpose in the next chapter.

3

TOWARD DIFFERENT ENDS

To start over, one thing we need is a new purpose of schooling, one that goes beyond citizen/worker binaries discussed in Chapter 1. I first provide an overview of traditional purposes of schooling and connect those to social, cultural, historical, and political contexts. There are several excellent and comprehensive historical accounts that I do not attempt to redo in this chapter (Gutmann, 1987/1999; Pinar, 1995; Spring, 2011). Rather, this brief discussion will give enough of a context to argue for a new purpose of schooling. I argue that the purpose of schooling should be *to facilitate human learning, meaning making, and knowledge production toward a just and equitable education for all.*

Purposes of Schooling

Schooling in the U.S. has many purposes; some even argue there are too many purposes—that we have placed too many demands on schools to meet social, cultural, and medical needs of our children and youth. Historically, we see a consistent binary of goals that vacillates between constructing good citizens or compliant workers. Sometimes we want both. In order to start over from a place of equality, we need a new purpose of schooling that is not just a balance of this old binary and one that does not simply add on more or "different" purposes to the traditional citizen/worker purpose. The traditional purposes of schooling, especially the unproductive citizen/worker binary argument, are outdated, have not provided a just and equitable education system, and do not recognize that all intelligence is equal; hence the need to start over with a new purpose.

Schools have been relied upon to regulate sexuality, reduce crime, improve children's health and nutrition (social welfare), and to manufacture and control community (Spring, 2011). It would be an understatement to say that we have an uneven record of fulfilling these goals given the controversies about who should decide what morals should be taught and whose welfare is of most worth. The recent banning of Mexican American studies in Arizona is but one example of what is at stake in schooling (Biggers, 2012) when what counts as "American" is in the hands of conservative politicians. In whose hands should this decision be? Where do "we the people" have a say in this decision? For whose good should we strive?

The founding of public schools in the U.S. has historically been linked to solving social problems identified by "society." Early social and political purposes of schooling sought to unite the ~~American identity~~ through common moral and political values ~~and a~~ common cultural identity in which the child was seen as the site of cultural conflict that schooling would resolve (Smith, 2003). Schools were sites for the "Americanization" of immigrants, for example. In the early twentieth century, schools were used to solve the "youth problem" by keeping them out of the labor market, and later in the twentieth century schools sought to produce racial and cultural harmony, and equality of educational opportunity (Spring, 2011). This latter purpose has not been achieved. We can see the interrelatedness of the citizen/worker binary through the twentieth century from Adler (1982) to deMarrais and LeCompte (1995); all of these perspectives connect school purposes to job preparation and citizen responsibility.

Historical purposes of schooling assume a similar kind of societal or common good in their articulation. That good is not decided upon by the "people" (May, 2010), but instead is decided by "society" vaguely defined. Traditionally the power elite described earlier has accomplished this task. Education has had a concern for the good of society since Aristotle, who argued that "the citizens of a state should always be educated to suit the constitution of their state" (Barker, 1958, p. 332). However, it is important to note that this position assumes a subjective purpose of education in which normative principles are determined and controlled by principles of a society, much like the ways in which Foucault (1991) described governmentality as the set of practices used to govern the self and others (Peters & Burbules, 2004).

Historically, we have seen political, social, and economic goals for what Spring (2011) calls the public good. Currently, the public good refers to economic good, which in neoliberal times means preparing for competition in a global economy. In this model, schools are to serve strategic national interests determined by local state and federal governments, much the same as argued by Plato. I am arguing that these claims and practices have failed to result in a just and equitable society—a public good—and thus we need to start over with assumptions of equality in which "we the people" would determine what counts as a common good (May, 2010).

The Common Good

Gutmann (1987/1999) outlined a typology of normative theories about the purposes of education that take the good of society into account. In a centralized state model put forward by Plato, what is good for the child is good for society. She argues that

> by teaching all educable children what the (sole) good life is for them and by inculcating in them a desire to pursue the good life above all inferior ones. They must realize their own good by contributing to the social good.
> *(Gutmann, 1987/1999, p. 23)*

"All educable children" is, however, problematic. Here is where we get issues of inclusion and exclusion that are typically determined through IQ and other forms of medical model evaluations that determine who is worthy of educating and that assume inequality of intelligence. However, if all intelligence is equally valued then I argue that *everyone* is worthy of educating and of educating in general education settings with appropriate supports. All intelligence is equal. No exclusions, no exceptions.

For others, education was in the hands of parents who, as the child's best teacher, have the right (obligation) to pass on their way of life to their children (Gutmann, 1987/1999). If the state was an individual, no one state/society decided on what constituted the good, rather individuals had the opportunity to choose what counts as the good life for themselves. Education was to offer the opportunity for children to choose freely and rationally among the widest range of possible lives. From this perspective, education provided a space to choose *the* good life or choose among a range of good lives with the choice being the individual's or the individual's parents. The problem is that there is no "the" that "we" think is good (not in pluralistic society) so we end up ceding the choice to governing bodies that determine what counts as the good life for us. These bodies then encode that idea into a set of institutional practices that may bear little resemblance to the idea of what constitutes "good"—the narrative is used to sell a set of practices and materials, what de Certeau (1984) would call strategies, that fulfill the governing body's goals. "We the people" are relegated to the role of consumer where we have no role in the production of that good life beyond what we might make do with within this strategic environment (de Certeau, 1984). Given assumptions that "our" society is worth carrying on, we have agreed by default to consciously reproduce what has come to be assumed as "the" good life, one that currently excludes poor people and people from non-dominant racial and cultural groups (Darling-Hammond, 2010), including people with disability labels and English learners.

Unfortunately, history has shown that what is considered beneficial usually ends up only being meant for *some* members of a community and we end up with policy people making decisions from a distance about who should be excluded. This tension over how decisions get made and who gets to decide has been attempted to be resolved in several ways: (1) choose the greatest good for the greatest number of people, or (2) the good is represented by the goal of the state to maintain order (Gutmann, 1987/1999). The second resolution privileges the individual's right to freely construct his/her life through reason and moral law (e.g., the interest of the state). Neither of these resolutions recognizes that whatever is defined as the common good needs to be understood as fluidly constructed in interaction, as radically context specific, and cannot be decided a priori. As long as we continue with modernist assumptions about rational mind, we will not see the changes we need to see in schools, or in the common good.

So what does the good life, or the common good in education, traditionally mean? Horace Mann (1848/1957) wanted the common school to bring together a diverse populace in ways that ameliorated difference. Society wanted schooling to include moral instruction to reduce crime and control behavior, and to eliminate class friction/divisions by mixing their children in schools (Spring, 2011). Thomas Jefferson (1784/1954) saw schools as places that would filter out the "rubbish" and produce leaders. These functions of school were seen as serving a common good determined by the leaders of the time—all White, able, male, slave owners. I am not sure adhering to decisions made by these men is morally defensible in a world in which all women, poor people, people from non-dominant groups, people with disability labels, and English learners are now understood to be worthy of educating, not as rubbish. As Fielding and Moss (2011, p. 15) suggest:

> The school has always been at risk of being a place of regulation and normalization, tasked with producing subjects fit for the purposes of the nation state and the capitalist economy; in today's case, that means the autonomous, flexible, calculating, self-regulating and high consumption subject required of advanced liberalism and globalized hypermarket capitalism.

However, there is more to being human that needs to be accounted for in schooling; that more includes the idea that humans now produse knowledge in unprecedented ways. Furthermore, children and youth are turning their intelligence elsewhere given that school purposes remain outdated and that the common good does not include them in ways that make sense to them given what they see and experience outside of school. We need a new purpose that takes into account those practices that are currently going on in "we the people's" everyday lives, not one that simply serves the purpose of a capitalist economy.

Following the "citizen" side of the school purposes binary, Gutmann (1987/1999, p. xii) proposes a deliberative democracy in which there is reciprocity among free and equal individuals who offer one another morally defensible reasons for morally binding laws in an ongoing process of "conscious social reproduction" (p. 14). The purpose in this model is to socialize a populace to follow rules as a means of political control through the social contract of schooling. This social contract moves beyond equalizing access to schooling toward the improvement of political and personal lives. The people are not objects of legislation but are subjects in the construction of and participation in a democracy through civic responsibility. Here the purpose of schooling is to cultivate the skills and virtues of deliberative citizenship in a context where educational authority is shared among parents, citizens, and professional educators (Gutmann, 1987/1999, p. xiv). However, students are the key missing members of the team who should shape schooling: they are only seen as objects to be shaped (May, 2010). Furthermore, as Biesta (2011, p. 152) suggests, deliberative democracy remains a socialization model wherein the assumption is that the democratic citizen is "a pre-defined identity that can simply be taught and learned." And it represents the citizen side of the binary I have already shown to be unproductive.

I am not arguing that we do not want a democratically responsible citizen. Rather, I am saying that we have not achieved this goal (cf. low voter turnout in U.S. elections). Continuing along the same road will not change the result. Biesta suggests a subjectification model of democratic learning in which learning "has to do with and stems from engagement with and exposure to the experiment of democracy" (2011, p. 152). Subjectification, then, works alongside the presupposition of equality as learners participate equally in the processes of democracy itself (May, 2010). This model is more in line with the kind of processes of learning and development argued for in this book. That is, all learners (teachers, students, parents, administrators, community members) learn by equipotentially participating in the processes of democracy themselves.

In all of these traditional purposes, the people commit to the allocating of educational authority in such a way as to provide its members with an education adequate to participate in democratic politics, to choosing among a limited range of good lives, and to sharing in the several subcommunities, such as families, that impart identity to the lives of its citizens (Gutmann, 1987/1999). However, the question remains about whether our allocation of authority has been handled in ways with which we continue to agree. Are we satisfied with how schools are working? What is the "common good" we seek in contemporary times? The economic goal of the "efficient worker" side of the school purposes binary has taken the lead again, but with the added emphasis of global competition. I cannot see how the efficient worker goal will result in a just and equitable education given our historical lack of success.

Neoliberalism has brought with it an emphasis on globalization and filling a global marketplace with competitive workers. Smith (2003) defines globalization

Still the same "purpose" of school

as a tension between the local and global or the "glocal" (Arnove & Torres, 1999). He argues that, in what he calls globalization one, free operation of the global market system is the primary means of solving social problems and of achieving the common good. Hence, we see the privatization of social systems such as schooling through discussion of education as a tradable good. The increase in charter schools and for profit schools indexes the rise of neoliberalism in education. Neoliberal policy emphasized testing and standards as a way of ensuring competition and demanded strict financial accountability, in ways not actually practiced in business, instead of focusing on what children and youth need to learn authentically in order to be fully and meaningfully human (Hursh, 2008; Postman, 1995; Smith, 2003). Lastly, fundamentalist calls for a retreat to the "basics" mask neoliberal efforts to homogenize curriculum (e.g., Arizona's banning of ethnic studies) in ways that hide a nostalgic American norm, a norm that does not exist. Economic goals re-emerge as a key purpose of schooling and as the public good.

Economic goals, equated with what counts as the common good, are related to equality of opportunity to gain access to wealth and class status in a competitive market (Spring, 2011). In this way, schools have become economic commodities in which any ideas of education as public responsibility or as sites for democratic and ethical practice are suppressed (Fielding & Moss, 2011). Schools are supposed to provide an even playing field from which "anyone," if they work hard enough, can be "successful."[1] Clearly this goal is not fulfilled, rather matters are worse: all children do not have equal opportunity to learn (Darling-Hammond, 2010), let alone have equal access to wealth. And sometimes equal is not enough. To be equitable, we need to accommodate past injustices and to acknowledge that the playing field is not even. Furthermore, this goal assumes a uniform social body (a "normal"), one easily controlled (Foucault, 1979), or anesthetized by the illusion of equal access.

We are further anesthetized by the glimmer of a test score. A high score on a standardized test now substitutes for the common good and is linked to global economic competition. High-stakes testing uses "scientific measurement to socially engineer equality of opportunity" (Spring, 2011, p. 61). Displaying that score reveals the panoptical (Bentham, 1791; Foucault, 1978) gaze of the state in its attempt to gain capital through compliant workers. The "authority" to which we have ceded our rights has determined that preparing workers for a global economy, even if we are not actually doing so, outweighs equality and justice. We need to change the endpoint from normative theories about wealth and global competition to well-being, meaning making, and knowledge production in an equitable and just society. I argued in Chapter 2 that we could achieve this through equipotential access to participation in meaning making and knowledge produsing activities and practices.

I am defining common good in general terms; that is, a common good is something shared and beneficial for all members of a community or group

(Wikipedia, 2011). I use Wikipedia here purposefully as a unique source for unpacking what "we the people" think is the common good since "we the people" are the authors. The process of constructing shared goals would be contested and often difficult, but this is what happens when humans work together with assumptions of equality of intelligence, and would be a key part of constructing what counts as shared, while allowing for dissensus (Rancière & Corcoran, 2010) and continued revision.

I suggest that all parties who have a stake in that good should construct the common good locally. As I will describe in Chapter 4, the parties involved in education of children and youth should include teachers, administrators, parents, community members, and, most importantly, children and youth themselves. Together, teams made up of these groups would construct the good toward which they are working and build the purposes of curriculum, instruction, and assessment from that starting point. This process does not assume consensus is possible. Conversely, conflict and disagreement, or dissensus, are key parts of the process of constructing the common good and assure that the common good will not become static.

That the common good and the curriculum are locally constructed does not over-determine schooling as exclusively local. In contemporary times, the global is in the local. With advanced Internet communication technologies, local schools are connected globally and the skills and practices associated with that connection would be reflected in the curriculum.

So far I have shown that the purposes of schooling in the U.S. range from those focused on developing a globally competitive workforce to those focused on developing democratic citizens. Additionally, I have shown that what counts as the common good has become a high test score. In spite of the variation in purposes and common good, the persistent goal of preparing for work remains. Recent neoliberal nuances to this hegemonic goal focus on competing in a global economy, as seen in the new Common Core Learning Standards mandates (Common Core, 2012a).

Operationalizing the Neoliberal Common Good

Developed by the National Governors Association Center for Best Practices (NGA Center) and the Council of Chief State School Officers (CCSSO), the Common Core Learning Standards are an attempt to establish a national set of unified educational goals and outcomes. They argue that in order to compete in a global marketplace (worker purpose) and to prepare students for college and careers (also a worker purpose), the nation needs a consistent set of national benchmarks so that "we" can know students will be adequately prepared no matter where they live (Common Core, 2012a). All of these goals work toward positioning the population to be competitive in a global marketplace without articulating what that global marketplace is or what being competitive or adequately prepared therein means (Larson, 2013). Furthermore, the primary beneficiaries of this "common" good are places like the Gates Foundation and Pearson, as well as other corporations who will supply materials for implementation. Gates is funding a series of curriculum mappings (https://commoncore.org/maps/) aligned with the Common Core while Pearson will publish the tests (http://commoncore.pearsoned.com). At least someone's market goals will be realized.

The close of the Common Core (2012a) mission statement below indexes how the purpose of schooling is defined in the standards:

> The Common Core State Standards provide a consistent, clear understanding of what students are expected to learn, so teachers and parents know what they need to do to help them. The standards are designed to be robust and relevant to the real world, reflecting the knowledge and skills that our young people need for *success in college and careers.* With American students fully prepared for the future, our communities will be best positioned *to compete successfully in the global economy.*
>
> *(Emphasis added)*

Economic purposes of schooling take precedence in these standards as evidenced by the goal to position students as competitive in a global economy. Also included is college and workforce readiness (e.g., preparation for adult life argued for by Bobbitt). We can see the hegemony of historical purposes as they resurface in contemporary "standards." State governments who are seeking to maintain their federal funding are requiring these standards. College and career readiness is a key feature of the Race to the Top federal policy, for example, and states have to indicate how they will meet this goal in order to get and keep their funding.

I want to be clear that I am not arguing that children and youth should not have equal access to college and the careers of their choosing; rather just the opposite—all children and youth have a right to equal access to these discourses of power (Morrell, 2008). I am arguing that global economic competitiveness, as a purpose of education and a common good, is wrongheaded and will not result in a just and equitable education system or society, or in readiness for college and career. Furthermore, I argue that the predominant discourses of power about achievement and global competition need to change in order to begin to achieve justice and equity. Our focus needs to be on human well-being, meaning making, and knowledge produsage, not on producing compliant workers and non-critical citizens (Biesta, 2011).

I have included two additional examples of purposes of schooling that may represent how national trends reflect the goal of economic competition and how they are enacted on local levels. One, the New York City Board of Education, represents large school districts, while the Rochester City School District (RCSD) (my local district) represents mid-sized districts.[2] Note that the traditional binary of worker/citizen is apparent in both (success in global economy—RCSD; get good jobs/productive, successful lives—NYC). Normative theories about the purposes of schooling are evidenced by the focus on a central goal that should be sought after by all.

The Rochester City School District's (2011) mission states clearly that its purpose of schooling relates to skills needed in a global economy:

> The mission of the Rochester City School District is to provide a quality education that ensures our students graduate with the skills to be successful in the global economy.

What those skills are is not determined from the mission but can be seen in the host of curricular documents and reform initiatives in the district. What we see is a focus on autonomous concepts of knowledge as testable skill. Literacy, for example, is defined as academic language that can be divided into its parts and taught in sequence. The district has implemented numerous reform models that use this skills-based view: Success for All, Reading First, Direct Instruction, America's Choice, to name a few. Similar strategies are used in the state's largest district, New York City.

The New York City Board of Education (2011) states the following as its mission:

> Helping students learn is the end goal of New York City public schools. We are committed to providing students a solid education so they can go to college; get good jobs; and lead productive, successful lives.

Here we do see focus on learning, but learning is then defined as what one needs to go to college and get good jobs—those skills needed to live productive and successful lives. It is a singular narrative with one direction—school to college to job = successful life—again focusing on the normative. We can see echoes of the Common Core Learning Standards in both of these districts' missions—college and career. All of these vision statements index Race To The Top given the language around college and career. This language illustrates New York State's conformity to federal funding mandates since successfully applying for RTTT funds and subsequent requirements in order to continue to receive over $600 million. These examples show how hegemonic purposes of schooling play out on the ground in missions and their subsequent curricula.

Normative Purposes

As I have shown thus far, contemporary schooling tends to have a singular, normative focus on a purpose of schooling as preparation for participation in a global economy (the good life) via college and career. The trajectory is normative in that it is expected that everyone follow the same path; deviation results in exclusion. As Foucault (1979) argues, normalization is a key technique of power that is implemented in schools, prisons, and other public institutions as a form of disciplinary power. Non-conformity is punished in a variety of ways (bad grades, suspensions, reprimands) that compare, differentiate, hierarchize, homogenize, and exclude. It is these punishment strategies that construct and maintain the norm. The costs, however, are unacceptable. In Rochester alone, my research has shown that deficit ideologies about African Americans "fitting" into the normative context of schools have constructed academic disadvantage (Irvine & Larson, 2007). Furthermore, the graduation rate of less than 50% speaks loudly to the level of damage being done (Democrat and Chronicle, 2013). I often tell my students that this sort of damage is what Foucault (1979) calls damage at the level of the soul. Such things simply are intolerable and must be stopped.

We know that a person has achieved this normative goal when she/he has scored above average on a standardized test. Standardization is the key here—sameness (Gutiérrez, 2007). This sameness is required in spite of the incredible diversity of human life. I depict this singular focus in Figure 3.1 below.

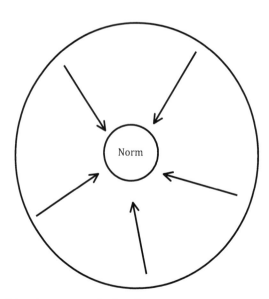

FIGURE 3.1 Traditional purposes of schooling

In this traditional view, schooling focuses on getting everyone to the central goal that is based on "normed" practices stemming from the early days of U.S. schooling when the idea was to assimilate students into a uniform citizenry and to weed out the rubbish (Jefferson, 1784/1954). We can argue about what that goal is, but research has shown that what it ends up being is for us all to conform to White, middle-class interactional and academic norms (Heath, 1982; hooks, 1994). This normative purpose is masked in high-resource schools that argue they cater to students' needs because those students most often represent the norm itself. The developmental trajectory for all students is unidirectional (toward the norm) and success is measured on standardized metrics that hold the norm constant.

A New Purpose

What I propose here is a different model wherein shared purposes are constructed in situ by local teams composed of students, teachers, administrators, parents/caregivers, and community members (see Figure 3.2). My proposed new purpose of schooling, *to facilitate human learning, meaning making, and knowledge production toward a just and equitable education for all,* removes a singular norm as each local

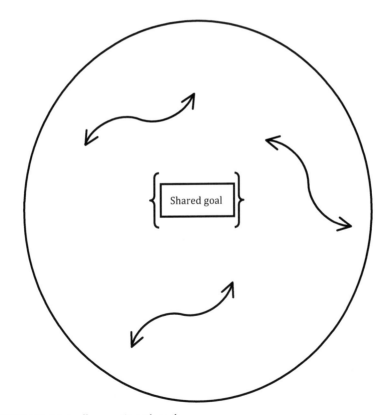

FIGURE 3.2 Mutually constituted goals

community constructs shared curricular, instructional, and assessment goals and purposes and would meet those purposes in ways they themselves construct. I am not simply talking about "bridging" home and school with this argument. Bridging metaphors assume a separation. In the model I propose, community members, parents, and other traditional non-school people (e.g., business owners) would be valued and authentic members of the school curriculum team that develops the purposes themselves, thus taking back their education. When all members count and are authentically included, we do not need a bridge.

In the view I am proposing, goals would be constructed by all parties involved and there would be multiple ways, or trajectories (the squiggly lines in Figure 3.2), to achieve that goal or goals through equipotential participation in the construction of shared purposes and curricular, instructional, and assessment practices. Everyone can take a different path toward the goal. Goals would be fluid, which would allow for the possibility to change the goal as the community itself changes or decides new goals are needed. Participants involved in constructing the shared goal/s, including students, will determine how we know the goal or goals have been achieved. In this way, we can account for multiple trajectories of learning. This accounting connects to the concept of equipotential participation in heterarchical structures that allow for multiple ways into the goal and for the goals to change.

The Freedom Market project described in Chapter 2 is one example of how a community might collaborate toward social justice ends in that they bring together multiple people and resources to transform their neighborhood. The Lunch Is Gross project shows what this collaborative construction of shared purposes would look like in a classroom. Gatto and her students constructed their goal (to change the lunches) and martialed a wealth of people and resources to accomplish that goal. In these ways, schools would be sites of mutuality, gathering places where information is prodused, shared, and radically deliberated among equal partners (including children and youth) and for shared purposes. The practices of study must be seen as "conversational, open-ended, and teleogically oriented to overcoming the alienation between human beings and between humans and the larger world" (Smith, 2003, p. 46).

This chapter has reviewed historical purposes of schooling and proposed that we need a new purpose if we are to remain relevant in the lives of U.S. children and youth and if we hope to achieve a just and equitable education system, certainly a worthy public good. I have proposed that a new purpose be *to facilitate human learning, meaning making, and knowledge production toward a just and equitable education for all*. This purpose moves away from economic or assimilationist motives and toward the view that human learning, meaning making, and knowledge production are valuable in and of themselves as educational goals. Furthermore, it privileges the goals of the community in which children and youth live rather than projecting a mythical "good life" that is only meant for some.

The following chapter outlines principles that would guide curriculum, instruction, and assessment that follow from the assumption that all intelligence is equal and that draw on this new purpose.

Notes

1 Successful is defined as a high test score.
2 It is the case that Rochester is one of New York State's "big five" districts and is thus "large" by comparison to the majority of other districts in the state. However, for my purposes and in relation to New York City and other massive urban cities like Los Angeles, Rochester represents "mid" sized districts.

4

CURRICULUM, INSTRUCTION, AND ASSESSMENT

How does a society educate across generations and what does it decide needs knowing? In the U.S., the answers to these questions have been shaped by the traditional curriculum question "What knowledge is of most worth?" This question has been answered by a number of entities and from a variety of perspectives, but most commonly in contemporary times it is answered by textbook companies who make a tidy profit when school districts purchase their elaborate curriculum packages (Larson, 2007). The Common Core Learning Standards movement is the most recent iteration of the answer to the traditional curriculum question. Together with high-stakes tests, these standards constitute what knowledge is valued. But who decides what counts as valuable to know? And who benefits from having the power to make this decision?

Power elites such as those assembled to establish the Common Core Learning Standards stand to benefit from having this power. They benefit by shaping what counts as valuable knowledge in ways that reflect their own ideologies about curriculum, teaching, and learning. Furthermore, textbook companies benefit financially. Given the profound changes in communicative practices in contemporary times discussed in Chapter 2, the curriculum question needs to be

> what kinds of things should we be learning and teaching now in order to prepare learners as well as possible for handling what comes in the future, *and* to be able to act better now as well as later in order to create more viable futures?
>
> *(de Alba et al., 2000, p. 12, emphasis in original)*

Yet, we still need to ask who will decide and whose interests are served by having this decision making power?

Currently politicians and business people are making these decisions and are eliminating teachers in the process. Students have not been a part of this discussion at all. Who makes the rules about what gets taught to whom? What are the implications for curriculum, instruction, and assessment if we start from a place of equality of intelligence rather than inequality? This is an important question given, as Rancière suggests, the pedagogical myth that the student can only understand when explained to. What will change when all intelligence is equal and knowledge is prodused rather than explained?

Building on the new ontological and epistemological foundations established in Chapter 2 and the new purpose of schooling in Chapter 3, I describe curricular and instructional principles that would guide curriculum development and implementation as one attempt to answer these questions. Moving beyond a narrow focus on high-stakes testing, I also articulate assessment principles.

Curriculum

Curriculum theories come and go with political waves of panic or shifting ideological positionings. If history has taught us anything, it is that curriculum is not neutral and that it is always grounded in ontological and epistemological theories that shape pedagogy, assessment, and policy (Kliebard, 2004; Spring, 2011). Those groundings are most often not articulated and, thus, become hegemonic assumptions about neutrality.

I usually explain what I mean by this to graduate students by connecting it to Gee's (2011) concept of big "D," little "d" discourse. With apologies to Gee, I identify big "C," little "c" curriculum. Big "C" curriculum has to do with the theoretical and ideological foundations of curriculum, the curriculum theory and its connections to social, cultural, historical, and political contexts. Little "c" curriculum is the content and pedagogy that follows from this foundation. Little "c" curriculum is usually the only thing teachers have access to and is what is "delivered" to students in traditional classrooms. The Common Core Learning Standards present the current little "c."

Standards are a derivative of the big "C" curriculum and are produced by "experts" who articulate the little "c" for teachers. Standards do not explicitly state their theoretical foundation, thus masking power relations and reducing that to which teachers have access to narrow goals only focused on instruction as explanation (lesson, units, and activities that meet standards). A typical standards document emphasizes what students will know and be able to do rather than explicitly stating the underlying theories of curriculum, teaching, and learning (traditional theories are explained in the next section). Teachers are expected to develop lessons that will accomplish the "know and be able to do" piece without knowing the "why." Increasingly, districts produce such lessons for teachers rather than rely on teachers themselves as experts.

TABLE 4.1 Anchor Standards

Key ideas and details

1. Read closely to determine what the text says explicitly and make logical inferences from it; cite specific textual evidence when writing or speaking to support conclusions drawn from the text.
2. Determine central ideas or themes of a text and analyze their development; summarize the key supporting details and ideas.
3. Analyze how and why individuals, events, and ideas develop and interact over the course of a text.

In current times, the Common Core Learning Standards are one answer to what U.S. society wants its youth to know; however, I argue it constitutes only the little "c" of curriculum. A closer look at the Common Core shows traces of *A Nation at Risk,* No Child Left Behind, and Race To The Top through their narrow focus on outdated skills. We can also argue that the technical/rational and academic core frameworks discussed in the next section remain the hegemonic base for the Common Core, given its focus on static notions of what counts as knowledge and its focus on transmission of knowledge as pedagogy.[1]

For example, in the Common Core Standards for English Language Arts (Common Core 2012b, p. 10) there are four "anchor" standards that include ten substandards. The first anchor standard is featured in Table 4.1. Note the use of directives framed in behavioral terms that position students and teachers as passive followers of these directives (cf. Bloom's 1969 taxonomy). Knowledge is in the text and the text is where the evidence is located. Given these linguistic markers, we can see how the Common Core reflects traditional transmission models of teaching and learning and assumes inequality of intelligence (people have to be told how to find evidence). Furthermore, the standards assume one answer to the directives posed and that answer is known by experts who will determine whether and how "the" answer is learned by the "unknower."

Following the articulation of the anchors, more detailed grade level specifications are listed (see Table 4.2) (Common Core, 2012b, p. 11). We can see traditional, autonomous concepts of reading as decontextualized skill (Street, 1995) in these standards that focus on meaning as contained within the text itself, and not in the interaction with the reader and author. And it appears there is only one interpretation available ("determine central message, lesson, or moral") that will most certainly be expected on the test that will be developed to assess these standards. Multiple ways of knowing and being are not accounted for, nor are the social and cultural practices of "reading" that students bring to the classroom.

TABLE 4.2 ELA Standards K-2

Kindergartners	Grade 1 students	Grade 2 students
Key ideas and details	Key ideas and details	Key ideas and details
1. With prompting and support, ask and answer questions about key details in a text.	1. Ask and answer questions about key details in a text.	1. Ask and answer such questions as who, what, where, when, why, and how to demonstrate understanding of key details in a text.
2. With prompting and support, retell familiar stories, including key details.	2. Retell stories, including key details, and demonstrate understanding of their central message or lesson.	2. Recount stories, including fables and folktales from diverse cultures, and determine their central message, lesson, or moral.
3. With prompting and support, identify characters, settings, and major events in a story.	3. Describe characters, settings, and major events in a story, using key details.	3. Describe how characters in a story respond to major events and challenges.

Source: Adapted from McNeil, 1990.

Historical Overview

There have been many typologies of curriculum ideology put forward (Pinar, 1995). I am not proposing another typology, but arguing instead that all are outdated. As de Alba et al. (2000, p. 8) claim:

> formal educational theory, policy, and practice with respect to curricular content and processes, skills, and knowledge is comprehensively outdated. It assumes and builds upon *categories* and *modus operandi* that no longer apply.
>
> *(Emphasis in original)*

As discussed in previous chapters, traditional educational theories and practices are based on faulty assumptions about how knowledge is produced and assume inequality of intelligence. These assumptions are no longer relevant in the age of advanced Internet communication technologies and mass collaboration.

Instead, we need curriculum that assumes equality of intelligence and that provides spaces for equipotential participation in the content decided by local teams.

> Any curriculum statement or theory must refer to *what* students are (expected) to learn and *how* they are expected to go about learning, *what* teachers are to teach and *how* they are to teach it. From a slightly different

perspective, we may think in terms of curriculum as having to deal with both the *structure* and *content* of knowledge.

(de Alba et al., 2000, p. 7, emphasis in original)

A curriculum theory consistent with the principles of equipotential participation, produsage, mass collaboration, and the sociality of space I have described needs to refer to what learners (including teachers) are to learn, how they are to learn it, and where and, most importantly, why. Furthermore, the theory needs to account for teachers, children, and youth as authors of curriculum.

Before moving to propositions about what C/curriculum follows from the principles articulated in Chapter 2, it is important to understand the history of the answer to the classic curriculum question about what knowledge is of most worth. Knowing where we have been helps us better understand where we need to go and what specifically needs to be transformed.

Historically, the structure and content of knowledge have been shaped by progressive philosophy that is manifested in a variety of ways in curriculum theory. The Progressives advocated the transformation of culture through the transformation of schools. Specifically, American Pragmatists such as Dewey (1899) argued that education involves a process of growth and critical transformation of the individual, then society. The educational extension of the Progressive movement produced several variations—positivism, humanism, and social reconstructionism, each with its own framework for curriculum. I turn to a brief discussion of these frameworks before moving into a discussion of what a new C/curriculum might look like. I have summarized the main points of the curriculum frameworks I describe below in Table 4.3.

Areas of Curriculum Theory

The *technical/rational or social efficiency* (Kliebard, 2004; McNeil, 1990) movement together with the focus on school subjects in the academic core (described next) serve as the hegemonic foundation of curriculum in U.S. schools today. As I mentioned, all curriculum is theoretically grounded in what I have called the big "C" part of curriculum. In the technical/rational model, following Enlightenment epistemologies about rationality and the scientific method, "C"urriculum is a rational system designed to control an efficient transmission of what "experts" have determined is worthwhile knowledge. Curriculum as little "c" is viewed as a neutral, technical matter, not a social, cultural, historical, or political one. Using ideas from industry about effective productivity and psychological views of teaching, learning is understood behaviorally as systematic, predictable, and testable (Bobbitt, 1918; Charters, 1909; Thorndike, 1913). Skinner's (1954) behaviorism became a model for sequencing learning tasks toward specific terminal behaviors (e.g., learning as observable behavior), wherein teachers elicited and rewarded correct responses. Because knowledge was viewed as static and rational, there was only one correct answer to questions. Tyler's rationale (1949), Bloom's Taxonomy (1969), Taba's (1962) lesson sequence, and Hunter's (1982) Seven Steps are all pedagogical tools rooted in this curriculum framework and are hegemonic practices in schools today. Key concepts that have grown out of the technical/rational framework that we currently take for granted as "neutral" educational givens include mastery learning, task analysis, and standardized testing.

The big "C" of the technical rational framework is rooted in positivism or the science of education that argues that science is the ultimate arbiter of truth and, as such, we must employ the methods of science to understand educational processes. Bobbitt, Charters, and Tyler respectively all drew heavily on positivism in the development of their curricular frameworks. In this view, the task of education was to transform society through science. A critical reading of these texts, however, leaves us with some questions. Cherryholmes (1988) puts it this way:

> The structural arguments of Tyler, Schwab, and Bloom et al. are based upon unstable categorical distinctions, take ideological positions while denying ideology, offer advice about correcting practice that reinforces practice in place, promote nonlinear structures as linear, advocate educational decision making separate from considerations of ethical or decision criteria, and ignore effects of power in discourse-practice. Why, one is led to ask, are such arguments widely cited if they do not do what they claim? Why are they privileged? If these arguments fail to do what they claim, what ends do they serve? They serve to reproduce educational practices in place in the name of change and progress.
>
> (p. 47)

In other words, they maintain the privilege of those power elites who control what counts as valuable knowledge and what counts as teaching and learning.

Calls for change have been prevalent since the beginning of common schooling in the U.S., and often hide the reproduction of the status quo. Complementary to, yet also a response to critiques of the content of the curriculum, was what has been called the Academic Core or Liberal Arts curriculum frameworks.

Academic Core (curriculum as worthwhile knowledge) and *Liberal Arts* frameworks are inextricably connected to the technical/rational, social efficiency models mentioned above, as they are based on the same ideological tenets. The Academic Core represents the content of the curriculum in which pedagogy is viewed as a neutral series of tasks through which content is "delivered." Together with the technical/rational framework they form the hegemonic content base of contemporary curriculum and policy discussions. The framework has been implemented under several different, yet related, names. For example, Bruner's (1960) Structures of the Disciplines viewed knowledge as justified belief where the primary goal was the development of the rational mind. Using the structure of academic disciplines such as science and math, he argued that the discipline's organizational structure determines the borders of inquiry, its substantive structure the kinds of questions that should be asked, and its syntactical structure determines the manner in which the data are gathered. Similarly, Hirst's (1974) Forms of Knowledge approach focused on mastery of the rational structure of knowledge forms that he determined to be mathematics and logic, physical (empirical) sciences, history and human sciences, aesthetics (literature and fine arts), morals, philosophy, and religion. That knowledge should be divided into content areas at all was a taken-for-granted assumption (Goodson, 1982).

In a liberal arts aspect of this framework, the so-called Great Books approach teaches cultural traditions from Plato to Rousseau using a specific body of approved texts that "experts" have determined are crucial for transmission to future generations. Hirsch (1987) builds on these ideas to form the Cultural Literacy approach that argued there is certain "common" knowledge necessary to participate in the U.S. culture and that this knowledge is factual. As factual, it can be bounded, sequenced, transmitted, and tested. Building on the ideologies of the Cultural Literacy approach, the Common Core Learning Standards (Common Core, 2012a) are one current example of what power elites have decided they want children and youth to learn in school that is rooted in positivist epistemology and technical–rational/academic core curriculum frameworks. The Common Core Learning Standards are still based on what students should know and be able to do in behavioral terms. By remaining focused on measurable behavior, curriculum stays at the little "c" level and continues to mask underlying ideologies.

Instead, the curriculum development teams I propose would use language that focuses on process rather than behavior to talk about knowing and doing, thus acknowledging a more fluid, anti-foundationalist stance on knowledge produsage. Curriculum ought to be fundamentally integrated (e.g., no separation of content areas or so-called "functional skills") and organized around issues, problems, and processes in broad units of study that afford maximum flexibility for teaching and learning. Gatto's (2013) unit of study that resulted in the *Lunch Is Gross* documentary is one example of what this might look like in practice in a classroom.

Humanism (curriculum as human growth) asks what it means to be human as its C/curriculum question. The answers focus on how curriculum can contribute to human growth and development. In this view, curriculum should provide personally satisfying experiences, support innovation, and self-discovery that are exploratory (McNeil, 1990). Concepts from humanistic psychology such as self-actualization and the importance of the affective self appeared in curriculum and pedagogy in such things as student-centered curriculum that emphasized student choice and relevance. The teacher served as the facilitator of individualized instruction in which learning was seen as personal growth and development.

The means-before-ends arguments in humanism contributed to important classroom implications through the development of authentic learning and assessment tools such as portfolios and other performance assessments. Humanism's tenets rose and fell according to political maneuverings around global competition for space (mid-twentieth century) and for the global marketplace (twenty-first century). When economic competition discourses rose in the larger society, a "back to basics" movement took over and we saw a fall back to technical/rational and academic core conceptions of what needs to be taught in schools. Each fall back move produced further entrenchment into hegemonic ideologies.

While Du Bois is not commonly associated with curriculum history, this is more an artifact of academic racism than the relevance of his work to the conversation about education in the U.S. At the beginning of the twentieth century, W. E. B. Du Bois (1902/2002) wrote about educational principles needed to effectively educate African Americans as part of the transformation of society. He was clear that to have education without power would not lead to self-determination or the ability of African Americans to be responsible for their own lives and destinies. Given that he was focusing on development and transformation, I would locate him in the humanist tradition of early curriculum theories.

Humanism's big "C" epistemological foundations grew out of Naturalism (child-centered movement where the child is viewed as an ideal) in which the best education is to provide an environment in which the child can flourish naturally as she/he is protected from the corrupting influence of society. From this perspective, the task of school is to transform society or overthrow the society vis-à-vis the child. In other words, transformation occurs by providing the child opportunities to take control and to learn experientially (Dewey, 1938).

Social reconstructionism (curriculum as societal transformation), while typically not taken up in schools, is an important curriculum framework that I build on later in this chapter. This framework examines the relationship between curriculum and the social, political, and economic development of society and is concerned with society as it should be as opposed to as it is (McNeil, 1990). Of course, the problem of who decides how society should be remains.

In a principal work, Counts (1932) embraced the idea of indoctrination as articulated in the assertion that the task of school is to reconstruct society and to prepare students to know "better." He argues that since all societies inculcate values in children, the question is not whether but what to inculcate. As a result, there are two choices: (1) modern feudalism or (2) economic democracy. He argues that clearly 2 is better than 1; therefore teachers ought to teach for economic democracy. Thus the answer to the classic curriculum question was economic democracy in which we organize society (schools) to protect ourselves from mistakes of those in power. In this view, the task of education is to recognize the mistakes made and correct them.

For social reconstructionists, the purpose of education is to confront learners with problems of humanity and to find ways to rectify them. Early social reconstructionists (Brameld, 1956; Counts, 1932; Rugg, 1936) viewed schools and curriculum as tools to create a more just and equitable social order. Rugg (1936), for example, used social criticism to challenge the values promoted in schools. Counts (1932), as I mentioned earlier, argued for the more active role schools could take in the creation of a new, more equitable society and that schools should inculcate these values in students. Brameld (1956) argued more specifically that schools should: (1) articulate a commitment to building a new culture; (2) promote the notion that workers should control the institutions and resources in order to have a true democracy; (3) empower the individual to understand her role as social planner; and (4) convince the learner of the value of social change. The role of the teacher was to relate national, world, and local purposes to students' goals in ways that challenged the beliefs of students and that developed their critical consciousness. Learning opportunities must meet three criteria: (1) they must be real, (2) they must require action, and (3) they must teach values (McNeil, 1990). Even more specifically, the instructional sequence should identify a problematic issue, examine realities of students' lives (including constraints and root causes), link issues to institutions and structures of larger society, relate social analysis to an ideal, and take action to bridge ideal and reality.

Yet all of these frameworks assume the inequality of intelligence and are based on delivery models of curriculum (e.g., Freire's banking model) where what should be known is decided by experts and is then "put into" the empty heads of learners who do not know. Critical theories help to move us closer to an understanding that all intelligence is equally valued, and are discussed next.

Shifting Toward the Critical

Critical curriculum theory builds on the work of the early social reconstructionists and is a further step to having a goal of curriculum to expose the tacit values that ground the enterprise of schooling. The underlying assumption is that the covert functions of schooling are rooted in a capitalistic economy that cannot provide for either an equitable society or an equitable school system. Critical theorists often regard themselves as revealing the covert assumptions and values in the social text (McLaren, 1994). Critical theorists are typically concerned with creating awareness of the ways in which an unequal and unjust social order reproduces itself through the schools (Bowles & Gintis, 1980). To achieve the goal of revealing covert assumptions requires an examination of the structure of schooling, the ways in which roles are defined, and the hidden messages that are taught, for example, through the hidden curriculum, or the tacit messages students receive in the process of schooling (Jackson, 1992). The principal curriculum question in this examination is: Whose interests are being served?

TABLE 4.3 Summary of Curriculum Frameworks

Academic core	Technical/rational	Humanism *Control*	Social reconstructionism
1. Structure of the disciplines (Bruner): • Knowledge as justified belief • Primary goal is the development of rational mind • Curriculum based on the structure of the academic disciplines • Organizational structure indicates borders of inquiry • Substantive structure indicates kinds of questions asked • Syntactical structure determines the manner in which data are gathered. 2. Forms of knowledge (Hirst): • Focuses on mastering fundamental rational structure of knowledge • Forms: mathematics and logic, physical (empirical) sciences, history and human sciences, aesthetics (literature and fine arts), morals, philosophy, and religion. 3. Liberal arts: • So-called Great Books approach • Teach the traditions from Plato to Rousseau. 4. Cultural literacy (Hirsch & Ravitch): • Certain knowledge necessary to effectively participate in national culture (memorizing facts) • Factual knowledge linked to culture (facts over process) • Common knowledge approach.	• Technical production of knowledge requiring the determination of ends before means • Curriculum is technical (neutral) not political matter • Learning is systematic, predictable, and testable • Productivity methods of industry used in education • Skinner's behaviorism: sequence learning tasks toward specific terminal behaviors, elicit response from learners to these tasks, and reinforce correct responses • Tyler's rationale, Bloom's Taxonomy, Taba's lesson sequence, and Hunter's Seven Steps • Concepts of mastery learning, task analysis, and standardized testing.	• Assumes the growth and development of humans • What does it mean to be human? How can this be developed? • Curriculum should provide personally satisfying experiences • Supports innovation and self-discovery through activities that are exploratory, puzzling, playful, and spontaneous • Self-actualization • Addresses affective self • Student-centered curriculum emphasizing student choice • Teacher as facilitator • Learning as personal involvement • Authentic learning and assessment (portfolios, performance assessment) • Concept of relevance becomes important • Individualized instruction and development • Means before ends.	• Examines the relationship between curriculum and the social, political, and economic development of society • Concerned with society as it should be as opposed to as it is • Purpose of education is to confront learner with problems of humanity • Schools should: (1) articulate a commitment to building a new culture; (2) promote the notion that workers should control the institutions and resources in order to have a true democracy; (3) empower the individual to understand her role as social planner; and (4) convince the learner of the value of social change • Learning opportunities must meet three criteria: (1) it must be real, (2) it must require action, (3) it must teach value • The instructional sequence should: (1) identify a problematic issue, (2) examine realities of student's lives (including constraints and root causes), (3) link issues to institutions and structures of larger society, (4) relate social analysis to ideal, (5) take action to bridge ideal and reality.

Source: Adapted from McNeil, 1990.

Bowles and Gintis (1980) launched a form of analysis rooted in a conception of the overpowering domination of capital that attempted to unravel certain political and economic injustices within education. They argued that the purpose of schools was to reproduce the social relations necessary for maintaining a market economy by creating passive workers who would adjust to the imperatives of the capitalist order. Bourdieu and Passeron (1990) also argued that school was essentially an institution whose mission is cultural reproduction. They brought forward a Gramscian perspective in which schools were said to create cultural capital for those who occupy positions of power as intellectuals within the cultural apparatus of the larger society. Dominant forms of cultural capital had a certain exchange rate on the market that was accessible to very few people (White, upper middle class, male). In other words, access to this cultural capital created the power elites discussed in Chapter 1.

The roots of these ideas are found in the work of Karl Marx on the alienation of labor. For Marx (1867/1977), the objective conditions of work defined the realities that workers experience, and when work was organized to provide profit to those who own the sources of production, the working class was inevitably exploited. The working class must, therefore, assume control of the sources of production and socialize the economy so that each individual received according to her needs and contributed according to her ability. Class and equality, then, were a function of economic conditions.

The work of Paolo Freire is foundational to contemporary critical theory in general and to critical literacy in particular (Morrell, 2008). In this work, Freire (1970) devised an approach to the development of literacy that was based on the deep-seated practical needs of students. Reading materials were texts whose words and context were directly related to the real world of work his students knew in their everyday lives. He used the students' newly acquired ability to read as a base from which to help them understand the conditions of their labor and the interests being served by their work. Freire introduced the concepts of *conscientization,* or critical consciousness, as learning to perceive the world and to take action to change the oppression and contradictions in it, and *praxis,* or action with reflection. Current research in what has been called the New Literacy Studies (Street, 1995) pushes this field of critical literacy (literacy as cultural capital) further by examining the assumptions of critical theorists in terms of how they define what it means to be literate/illiterate and how Western-dominated conceptions of literacy marginalize other definitions and uses of literacy.

These historical roots lay the groundwork for contemporary critical theorists who look specifically at unequal power relations in schools and how these relationships and ideologies produce and perpetuate unequal distribution of cultural capital based on race, class, and gender inequities found in the larger society (Apple, 1990; Giroux, 1983; McLaren, 1994; Morrell, 2008). This distribution, they argue, is regulated by the schools and feeds workers trained to fill certain, predetermined roles in a capitalist economy. Critical feminists expand critical theory by articulating the notion that critical pedagogists must acknowledge their own subjectivities in the recognition of their own place of privilege when examining schools (Ellsworth, 1989; hooks, 1994). Weiler (1988), for example, bases her interpretation of feminist methodology on Freire's notions of contextualizing curriculum to the sociopolitical context in which the teacher finds her/himself. The emphasis is on the analysis of texts for evidence of inequalities and injustice. The students then work to devise ways in which to take action against the status quo. Moreover, she argues that teachers must also recognize their own position of advantage in relation to the students when attempting to construct a relevant, action-oriented curriculum. Critical feminists articulated the notion that there are other ways of knowing than linear, cognitive models that are assumed to be universally applied to all. They also bring the idea of the primacy of relationships, i.e., society as related groups of people, not just individuals, and the notions of silencing and voice to the conversation on schooling. Traces of all of these historical discourses remain in schools today, although most curricula remain rooted in the technical/rational and academic core models.

In spite of the robustness of critical theories and the research that has emerged using these paradigms, we still do not have a just and equitable education system. Even chronologically "new" theory and policy maintains a focus on economic competition, only now it is global. Testing regimes still rule the day but in more insidious ways. Through the attachment of high stakes such as graduation to standardized tests, neoliberal policies that focus only on economic purposes of schooling undermine critical stances.

Perhaps there is a role for a different theoretical paradigm, one that acknowledges the socially constructed nature of knowledge and learning, but that also moves to decenter the subject to a position that focuses more on being in equipotential relation to others and to other social constructs instead of being positioned as the "norm" to which all "others" must conform. Poststructural curriculum theory might offer such a lens and would be complementary to the frameworks described in Chapter 2 because it acknowledges multiple ways of knowing and being.

I argue that there is a role for other kinds of basics that include a deep understanding of cultural history and present as an underlying platform from which we operate and build new knowledges. However, we need a more fluid concept of what counts as knowledge and learning, and we need to understand multiple ways of looking at the world rather than seeing only preset and static "bodies" of knowledge. Poststructuralism helps us change metaphors from skills to practices and from packages to networks. Building on the critical historical work just described and on the principles described in Chapter 2, I will draw on poststructural epistemologies as a foundation, the big "C," for the curriculum principles articulated in this book.

A Poststructural Turn

A poststructural lens interprets traditional curriculum as an authoritative discourse (Bakhtin, 1981) that normalizes content and skills and that assumes a modernist view of knowledge as static. Lyotard (1979/1989) talked about the modern as any science that legitimizes itself through grand narratives, or those stories cultures tell themselves about the world and how it works. A poststructural curriculum view suspects all grand narratives and understands that curriculum is a fluid, constantly changing discursive production (Cherryholmes, 1988).

Poststructuralist Curriculum Framework

To begin with, poststructuralism denies all appeals to foundational, transcendent, or universal truths or metanarratives and, as such, constitutes a radical break from Enlightenment epistemology that underlies traditional theories. Poststructuralism is a response to those theories that purported to discover invariant structures in society, the human psyche, consciousness, history, and culture (Peters & Burbules, 2004; Pinar, 1995). Both an assault on and outgrowth of a structuralism that sought to identify the systems that create meaning, poststructuralism has sought to repudiate, dismantle, and reveal the variance and contingency of those systems (Pinar, 1995). de Alba et al. (2000, p. 8) articulate the following sets of concepts in Table 4.4, associated with postmodern and poststructural curricular frameworks.

TABLE 4.4 Poststructural Principles

Anti-foundationalism	• Suspicion of transcendental arguments and viewpoints • Suspicion of metanarratives • Rejection of canonical descriptions and final vocabularies • Perspectivism and multiplicity.
Post-epistemological standpoint	• Rejection of the picture of knowledge as accurate representation • Rejection of truth as correspondence to reality • Standpoint, nonfoundational, or "ecological" epistemology.
Anti-naïve realism	• Anti-realism about meaning and reference • The nonreferentiality of language • The naturalizing tendency in language • The diagnosis and critique of binarism.
Anti-essentialism and the self	• The critique of the metaphysics of presence • Substitution of genealogical narratives for ontology • The cultural construction of subjectivity • The discursive production of the self • Analysis of technologies of self.

(Continued)

TABLE 4.4 (Continued)

Analysis of power/ knowledge	• The critiques of the metaphysics of presence • Questioning of the problematic of the humanist subject • Substitution of genealogical narratives for ontology • The cultural construction of subjectivity • The discursive production of the self • Analysis of technologies of self.
Boundary crossing	• Erasure of boundaries between literature and philosophy • Interdisciplinarity and multidisciplinarity.

Source: de Alba et al., 2000. Used with permission.

These principles afford us a lens through which to critique traditional curriculum as an oppressive metanarrative that needs changing in ways that will account for multiple ways of knowing and being in contemporary society. In this view, everyone can participate and everyone counts since all ways of knowing can be valued and all intelligence is equal.

Discourse[2] is a key concept in poststructural thinking. In a critique of structuralism's view of language, poststructuralists argue that discourse, which includes knowledge, and reality are mutually constructed rather than existing a priori as separate entities (Britzman, 2003; Derrida, 1967/1976; Foucault, 1978). This definition affords a shift from questions about who has power/knowledge to how and under what conditions particular discourses come to shape (and be shaped by) reality. If power is a function of discourse, then the very ability to define or unify or totalize phenomena is an act of power, as is any appeal to transcendental signifiers, metanarratives, foundations, or origins. The signifier is freed from the signified to become a free-floating signifier that can be defined only by other signifiers (Derrida, 1967/1976). In other words, meaning is always radically context-specific. Discourse is an historically and socially contingent practice which itself forms the objects of which it speaks (Foucault, 1978). Lyotard (1979/1989) argues that postmodern society is a knowledge society in which the individual subject is lost, being replaced by multiple selves, multiple intelligences, multiple surfaces, and fragmentation. What we know of the past can only be that which exists now and what we know can only be known through current representations (e.g., history is in the present).

We need to understand that discourse also positions and thus we need to be vigilant about that positioning and who might be marginalized or privileged therein. To quote Britzman (2003, p. 39) at length:

> Every curriculum, as a form of discourse, intones particular orientations, values, and interests, and constructs visions of authority, power, and knowledge. The selected knowledge of any curriculum represents not only things to know, but a view of knowledge that implicitly defines the knower's capacities as it legitimates the persons who deem that knowledge important.

This capacity to privilege particular accounts over others is based upon relations of power. Consequently, every curriculum authorizes relations of power, whether it be those of the textbook industry and demographics, established scholars, business and industry, specific traditions of knowledge or theories of cognition and human development.

What I argue here is that the curriculum and its associated relations of power that are currently in place have resulted in an unequal and unjust educational system. I do not see that changing unless we change fundamental assumptions about who and what counts for knowledge, learning, curriculum, and justice.

C/curriculum

If Poststructuralism becomes the new big "C" curriculum as we start over, then what follows as little "c"? As I described earlier, we need a curriculum that assumes all intelligence is equal and in which all parties are capable of equipotential participation. The curriculum should offer opportunities to build new ways of seeing the world rather than a simple transmission of predefined content and skills that are still rooted in assembly line curriculum ideology (de Alba et al., 2000; Pinar, 1995). We need both construction and deconstruction in order to stay relevant and fluid in the context of everyday life (Cherryholmes, 1988). Curriculum developers, teachers, and education researchers need to account for new ways of constructing and sharing knowledge that have developed with advanced Internet communications technologies that assume a level of participation for which traditional "basic skills" are background to semiotic manipulation and mobility, innovation, produsage, and many-to-many communicative structures. What might count as "basic" has drastically changed.

Using this perspective, curriculum teams that include teachers, administrators, parents, students, and community members would construct a district or school's curriculum, both big and little "c," using standards they determine to be relevant and meaningful to their community goals. In this way, standards are not eliminated (we need to have appropriate and situationally relevant goals), but those standards need to be decided upon with the curriculum teams and be connected to both local and global goals. The metaphor of the platform emerges as one way to think about curricular foci. As de Alba et al. (2000, p. 9) state, "The learner who masters 'platforms' can proactively generate interpretations and frame designs that in turn generate their own learning and innovation agendas and, ultimately, worldviews." It is the construction of such platforms that is the work of curriculum development—of developing ways to show intelligence to itself while accounting for disciplined inquiry. Curriculum teams would construct robust scenarios ba in poststructural platforms and analyze the word and the world (Freire & Mac 1987) in light of those scenarios. Scenario planning thus becomes one for curriculum development.

Scenario Planning as Curriculum Development Process

de Alba et al. (2000) propose the concept of scenario planning as a process to develop curriculum in the present that will prove sufficiently robust over several possible futures in ways that will critically engage learners. To use scenario planning, curriculum teams need to identify a question that is important to the community, after which they name driving forces that operate within and in relation to that question and how they are likely to play out over time given what they know now. Then they identify less known variables that could play out in different ways over time. Finally, they identify "critical uncertainties" (Rowan & Bigum, 1997, p. 81 cited in de Alba et al., 2000) that seem important but whose direction or influences are unknown in the present. de Alba et al. (2000, p. 17) give a number of examples of possible scenarios, one of which deals with the processes of globalization. I chose this one to explore, given that current discourses of globalization are so prominent. I argue that the question guiding this scenario focuses on what we need to know now that will help us cope with society as it may be in a plausible future (the guiding curriculum question). They articulate the scenario and its possible alternatives in Table 4.5.

TABLE 4.5 Scenario Planning for Alternative Globalizations

Globalization	*Agenda for alternative globalizations*	
• World economic integration with technological changes in telecommunications, information, and transport • (Political) promotion of free trade and the reduction in trade protection • Weakening of the nation-state and growth of local mafias, especially in former Eastern Bloc countries • Decline of the state and growth of multinationals brings a growing importance of the city (and hinterland) as the political administrative and governing unit • Imposition of structural adjustment policies on Third World countries	Promoting and developing a global social contract	• Promoting sustainable development • Promoting ecological standards • Consolidating the democratic process • Enhancing development of international labor markers • Promoting world trade union rights • Monitoring the social dimension of global and regional trade agreements.

(Continued)

TABLE 4.5 (Continued)

Globalization	Agenda for alternative globalizations	
• Emergence of a one-superpower hegemony but also the consolidation of China and world Islamization • Growth of religious and ethnic nationalisms • Increased gaps between richer and poorer, in terms of both economic and cultural/informational capital • Instability of the unregulated global financial system (financial collapse of the Asian "tiger" economies and economies of Soviet Union and Brazil).	Promoting and encouraging global governance	• Building standards of global governance • Protecting the public institutions of civil society • Developing transparency and accountability of international forums and world institutions • Developing approaches to institutions of an international civil community • Encouraging greater North/South dialogue and better world representation.
	Promoting and developing cultural globalization	• Promoting cultural diversity and exchange • Developing genuine multicultural structures and processes • Promoting and enhancing the notion of cultural rights • Protecting indigenous property rights • Promoting political and cultural self-determination.

Source: de Alba et al., 2000. Used with permission.

This scenario might be used to develop robust inquiry units, for example, that critically examine the potential consequences of globalization on government, geography, the economy, the environment, and knowledge production across disciplines. Meaningful links across content areas such as science (environmental concerns) or math (economy) that challenge learners (teachers and students) to produse new knowledge and new discourses about possible futures would also be developed.

The idea here is to think in terms of themes and of problem solving rather than static content or "critical thinking" skills. The question becomes what sorts of things must teachers and students know in order to thoroughly examine the alternative scenario? For example, what do we need to know now in order to "promote and enhance the notion of cultural rights" in the future, to take one example from the above scenario? How should we define culture and cultural rights? Who should decide this? The answers to these questions and the kinds of possible scenarios developed are only limited by the innovative thinking of the curriculum teams who are imagining possible futures for their community.

Some people might wonder what happens to the historical knowledge that society has agreed we want our children to know. What are those things? In math, this typically includes basic math functions and some higher order functioning up to algebra. After that, people move into specializations. In science, it is the scientific method, some chemistry and biology, and some basic "facts" (such as gravity). In English, it is "proper" grammar, some composition skill in a conventional sense, some interpretive capacity in poetry and literature, and knowledge of the literature "canon." Social studies are where we get citizenship education, workings and functions of government, and history (mostly as facts, dates, and historical figures). All of these can come to bear in the above scenario developed by local curriculum teams as they relate to problems that are identified by the community itself. The discussion in Chapter 2 of Lunch Is Gross and the Freedom Market are examples of groups of people positing alternative future scenarios and taking action to accomplish them. Gatto and her students imagined a healthier lunch and more equitable food practices across communities and brought literacy, science, math, and social studies to bear in their problem solving. The Freedom Market team imagined a community working toward economic independence and its resultant healthier populace. All traditional "content" was needed as they accomplished their work. In neither example were they constrained by static notions about "basic" standards and knowledge or about how they would test what was learned; they were concerned about the health and well-being of their communities.

A Different Scenario

More than content area points, however, "society" sees schools as places to "transmit" what humans have come to know, to socialize the young into acceptable behavior, and to produce efficient workers. If we begin with assumptions of equality of intelligence and take the new purpose of schooling to be *to facilitate human learning, meaning making, and knowledge production toward a just and equitable education for all,* then what little "c" results?

I propose that curriculum teams composed of teachers, administrators, students, parents, and community members use a problem-posing pedagogy and scenario planning to develop curriculum that would account for all intelligence being equal. By working together, the team would account for all ways of

FIGURE 4.1 Curriculum design frameworks

knowing and being as they examine their local context for issues and/or problems that need solving. If they do not have present "problems" in a community,
they could look to literature and history to find problems humans have encountered over time and figure out how they dealt with them and do some analysis
about those solutions. Then scenario planning would work for future oriented
curricula. We could use an historical problem–present problem–future problem
model of curriculum development into which we articulate a variety of possible scenarios, as shown in Figure 4.1. Bidirectional arrows are used purposely
to account for the fluidity between time and space and the significant overlap in
"problems" over time.

   In sum, C/curriculum is currently based on outdated assumptions about
knowledge and knowledge production. The Common Core Learning Standards
are simply a continuation of the same wrongheaded assumptions, and they will
not result in the kind of educated populace they expect, nor will they result in
a just and equitable system. I argued that a poststructural view takes into account
that knowledge is socially constructed and that all intelligence is equal. I presented
scenario planning as one way to account for equipotential participation and
knowledge produsage as curriculum planning teams come together to imagine
alternative futures.

"Instruction" and Pedagogy

Traditionally, educators define instruction as the "how" of curriculum delivery
(Doyle, 1992). The method of delivery becomes pedagogy or what Rancière
would call explication. Britzman (2003, p. 54) argues "pedagogy points to the
agency that joins teaching and learning." Cherryholmes (1988) describes
instruction as what results when teachers confront the pragmatics of the classroom, students, and content. Shulman's (1987) model defines instruction as
the tools of pedagogical content knowledge in the delivery of curriculum that
include activities such as presentations, speech acts like questioning, and varying
grouping strategies. However, the word "delivery" itself belies traditional
concepts of knowledge as outside of human interaction, or as something that
can be put into a person. Problematizing this concept is a key step in starting
over.

In spite of reforms and extensive research, a dominant set of instructional practices remains entrenched in U.S. schools: whole class instruction, lecture, known-answer questions, and an over-reliance on textbooks (Cuban, 1994; Gutiérrez, 1995; Mehan, 1979; Shannon, 1989). The concept of instructional delivery through a set of normalized practices forms the hegemonic base of what counts as instruction in contemporary schooling. These practices are based in a theory of learning that assumes the simple transmission of knowledge into empty brains and assumes inequality of intelligence.

These models are fundamentally flawed in that they rest on the assumptions that knowledge is static, that it exists outside human interaction, that it can be transmitted from one head to another, and "separates knowledge from experience and experience from the knower" (Britzman, 2003, p. 51). Furthermore, the concept of instructional delivery itself assumes the inequality of intelligence and fulfills Rancière's myth of pedagogy by assuming unidirectionality—from the knower to the unknower. We have known for a long time, at least since Berger and Luckmann (1967), that knowledge is socially constructed and that it cannot be put into empty heads since heads are never empty. Given that pedagogy and learning cannot be separated, we need a theory of learning that moves beyond behaviorism to account for the social construction of knowledge and the equality of intelligence.

Pedagogy and Learning

Sociocultural theory has articulated another way to think about learning, one that comes closer to seeing all intelligence as equal. From this perspective, people learn by jointly participating in the valued cultural practices of their communities (Gutiérrez & Rogoff, 2003; Larson & Marsh, 2005; Rogoff, 2003, 2011; Vygotsky, 1978, 1986). Learning occurs through participation in social, cultural, and historical practices that are mediated by interaction. Rogoff (2008) clarifies the complexity of participating in cultural practices by thinking about participation as occurring on three mutually constituted planes: apprenticeship, guided participation, and participatory appropriation. All occur simultaneously but can be foregrounded for analytic purposes. Apprenticeship corresponds to the plane of community activity in which experts (they could be teachers or students in the case of schools) arrange the occurrence of learning activities and regulate the difficulty of tasks to facilitate learning. By modeling expert performance during joint participation in activity, knowledge and learning are jointly constructed. Guided participation refers to interpersonal processes occurring in activity in which experts orient the learner to the task, provide links between what is known to what is not yet learned, and structure the activity so as to afford the learner a range of learning choices, with their roles collaboratively adjusted so that they are involved at a level that is challenging but within reach (e.g., within their zone of proximal development[3]). Participatory appropriation corresponds to personal processes in which the learner changes through participation in activity and indicates how that participation prepares the learner for future similar activities. With equipotential participation, however, children and youth are more than "objects" of participation as they shift to subjects of meaning making and curriculum development in collaboration with others. In this way, learning occurs on the three planes for all present and does not have to be determined only by adults.

One might think of the cultural practices as the "content" of learning. The child is an active member of a constantly changing community of learners in which knowledge constructs and is constructed by larger cultural systems. The active nature of the learning process implies that knowledge construction is mutually constituted (Cole, 1996). The dual process of shaping and being shaped through culture implies that humans inhabit "intentional" (constituted) worlds within which the traditional dichotomies of subject and object, person and environment, and so on cannot be analytically separated and temporally ordered into independent and dependent variables (Cole, 1996, p. 103).

A Focus on Culture

Of particular significance is that sociocultural theory presents a culturally focused analysis of participation in everyday life, in both formal and informal learning settings. As such, it offers researchers and other educators a way to meaningfully use children and youth's cultural resources as valuable for curriculum (Gutiérrez & Rogoff, 2003; Lee, 2001; Moll, Amanti, Neff, & Gonzales, 1992). This is a resource view rather than the deficit view that is common in schooling now. As Moll (2000) suggests, this view of learning helps us to see how children "live culturally" rather than isolating culture from the practice of everyday life. Power relations are also changed in that it constitutes a shift from traditional teacher-centered or student-centered classrooms (concepts familiar to most teachers) to conceiving of classrooms as learning-centered in ways that position both teachers and students as learners (Rogoff, 1994) and in which power relations, while asymmetrical, are more fluid and equitable. These principles align with the frameworks of equipotential participation and mass collaboration articulated in Chapter 2, and the poststructural curriculum framework described previously in this chapter, by clearly outlining the social origins of learning.

Social Origins of Learning

Once we make the shift to understanding that knowledge is socially constructed and learning happens in interaction with others, we can shift our ideas about pedagogy and instruction. Feminist pedagogy (Luke & Gore, 1992; Weiler, 1988), culturally relevant pedagogy (King, 1994; Ladson-Billings, 1995), and critical pedagogy (Kincheloe, 1993; McLaren, 1994) are pedagogies that begin from assumptions about the socially constructed nature of knowledge and learning and assumptions about the equality of intelligence. In these models of instruction, all members of the learning community are valued and their cultural practices incorporated into pedagogy in meaningful ways. We can see a place for equipotential participation where everyone counts as a valuable contributor to ongoing activity in these models.

If, as Rancière suggests, all intelligence is equal and learning does not require explication, what further changes do we need in pedagogy? What changes about "instruction" (pedagogy) when the fundamental premise is that learning does not require explication? To answer these questions we need to conceive of learning as a process of emancipation within which pedagogy becomes the process of showing intelligence to itself through shared construction of purposes of curriculum and of the curriculum itself. In this way, learning happens for all parties (teachers, students, parents, administrators, community members) through joint participation in curriculum development, implementation, and assessment that are situated in contexts of use. Power would circulate fluidly in heterarchical social relations in which no one person holds power as participants produse new knowledge rather than have old knowledge instructed and tested. There would be more than one "correct" answer (correctness is relative); however, there would still be a role for expertise even when there is no "correct" answer. Classroom discourse structures need to be flexible in order to accommodate multiple forms of participation and expertise. In other words, classrooms should use responsive/collaborative scripts (Gutiérrez, 1995). Answers that do get constructed would be rigorously grounded in empirical study.

Both of the examples in Chapter 2 exemplify these principles. For Gatto and her students, intelligence came to see itself in the process of producing the film. Everyone learned through participating, power was shared, and new knowledge prodused. There was no correct answer to the problem of school lunches, thus everyone's "answer" counted. Similarly, the Freedom Market showed how people came together to live the change they wanted to see and to learn together what those changes needed to be. No one person was in charge of what counted as authentic change.

Given these changes in curriculum and pedagogy, how might we know learners have learned? How will we assess?

Assessment

In simple terms, assessment implies the means by which we know that learners have learned what we want them to learn. In the current system, this means we want to know if they have learned what we "taught" them, pointing again to the inequality of intelligence and the myth of pedagogy. I discuss how assessment could be different when we assume equality of intelligence and equipotential participation later in this section. First, I present some current understandings about assessment as measurement.

Presently, assessment relies on measurement to try to determine what knowledge students possess (Popham, 2004). The idea that knowledge can be "possessed" assumes that knowledge is a static body that exists outside of human interaction and meaning making rather than being constructed in interaction. Furthermore, we are faced with the dilemma of deciding what, or whose, knowledge is worth "possessing" and then measuring. As Murphy (2012, p. 563) suggests,

> assessments, by virtue of their design, define the ways in which knowledge is represented and, in doing so, allow for some representations of knowledge while disallowing others. *Every* assessment is marked by limitations in design because no design can serve all possible functions. All assessment designs, in that sense, are flawed; they offer a view of learning but they are also marked by a lack of completeness. Epistemically responsible assessment is based on the premise that both the potential *and* the lack or limits of assessment are foregrounded in thinking about assessments and their consequences.

> *(Emphasis in original)*

What seems to be happening now is that assessment has become consumed by summative evaluation and the role of formative assessments forgotten in its design and implementation (William, 2000), hence the lack of completeness Murphy suggests. The pervasive demand for measureable outcomes has been reduced to high-stakes tests in which what counts as evidence is a test score (Popham, 2004). What counts as credible evidence indexes current measurement ideology that relies on modernist notions of the "true" (Mislevy, 1997). In other words, there is one truth, one right answer to questions, which can be evaluated and measured. Popham attributes the obsession with assessment as evaluation to hyperspecialization between the fields of curriculum, instruction, and assessment wherein each field operates in a silo. Maintaining disciplinary boundaries has overcome valuing authentic learning.

Obsessions with Measurement

The exclusive focus on measureable outcomes has divorced assessment from learning (William, 2000) and engendered a reductionist curriculum that harms children (Popham, 2004). We know from research that "reliance on a single test for repeated testing can distort instruction and lead to inflated and non-generalizable estimates of student gains in achievement" (Linn, 2000, p. 6), yet the obsession remains. Only those aspects of learning that can be measured are deemed worthy, harkening back to early scientific claims about representations of the "truth." The testing obsession seems to be useful politically and an inexpensive way to claim one is "doing reform." As Linn (2000, p. 6) suggests, "Tests are relatively inexpensive compared to other reforms, easy to mandate, can be implemented quickly and results are highly visible." Visibility is a key means of ensuring testing is valued since scores are now posted on the classroom door and published in the newspaper. However, we also know that no "score" can account for the complexity of human learning (Mislevy, 1997).

Why an obsessive focus on achievement defined as a test score? Achievement means accomplishing something; where did the test score come from? One source of the overemphasis on testing comes from IQ testing and its rather nefarious original purposes to separate humans along intelligence lines. Dixon-Román (2010, p. 98) argues that

> this cultural logic is embodied in the policies and *tools of legitimation* (i.e. standardized assessments) of the educational system. The use of mental testing in order to legitimate the intellectual superiority of the dominant culture has evolved into the use of standardized assessments in order to evaluate, sort, and hierarchize students on levels of ability and competence. Hence, there has been a continued focus on educational difference in order to support the ideals of advanced capitalism of competition, efficiency, and rugged individualism.
>
> *(Emphasis in original)*

Intelligence testing began in the 1900s when Binet was asked to determine which children would need help in schools. In spite of arguments made about the complexity of intelligence, Lewis Terman adapted the original test into the now popular Stanford-Binet Intelligence Scale (Roid, 2011), first published in 1916, and used on a large scale for the first time in World War I to determine appropriate military career tracks. What is often not mentioned is that Terman was a prominent eugenicist, which impacted his focus on identifying the less "able" (Leslie, 2013). Education has imported these ideas implicitly by continuing to use intelligence and other norm-referenced testing as acceptable measures, ignoring the explicit goal of separation of intelligence for purposes of exclusion (Ladson-Billings, 2011). This decision pushes beyond inequality of intelligence to the separation of intelligences that has resulted in inequalities, especially for poor children and children from non-dominant groups, including students with disability labels and English learners.

While college or career entrance exams have been in place for many years, using standardized measures to determine school and career tracks is relatively recent. The Elementary and Secondary Education Act of 1965 required proof of achievement in the form of a test score and represented a shift from the use of tests to determine need/track to the use of tests to determine academic success (Linn, 2000). The rise of accountability discourses in the 1990s raised the stakes of standardized testing (Linn, 2000) that has resulted in the high-stakes testing environment in which we find ourselves at the beginning of the twenty-first century. As Linn suggests, "Assessment systems that are useful monitors lose much of their dependability and credibility for that purpose when high stakes are attached to them. The unintended negative effects of the high-stakes account-ability uses outweigh the intended positive effects" (p. 14). This focus on effi-ciency and measurement harkens back to the social efficiency movement in the early twentieth century (Kliebard, 2004). Furthermore, it is a response to calls for competition in a global marketplace—a goal I have argued has not resulted in a just and equitable educational system for *all* children and youth.

Power and Discipline

We can see Foucault's (1979) disciplinary power at work in the surveillance of testing which tracks individuals to determine grade progress and spatial location (which school or classroom). From this perspective, students are judged by "professionals," through test scores, grades, and truancy laws to be worthy of inclusion or slated for exclusion in the form of special education, of being "pushed out" of school altogether (Fine, 1991), or tracked for higher achieve-ment (cf. Jefferson's searching for leaders). These techniques of disciplinary power are enacted through such visibility strategies as posting test scores on classroom doors and publishing school report cards in newspapers and online. The purpose of schooling here represents the social goal to control the population and to develop self-regulation (Spring, 2011).

These power relations have remained remarkably stable over the years, in spite of multiple attempts at reform (Gore, 1998). As Gore has pointed out, "pedagogy, as a modernist enterprise, has some continuous features across quite different locations" (p. 245). She found that techniques of power (surveillance, normalization, exclusion, classification, distribution, individualization, totaliza-tion, regulation) were prevalent at the interactional (micro) level in the varied settings of her research. Foucault's notion of power as capillary helps us see that while these techniques are prevalent and asymmetrical, they are not always oppressive. However, I would argue that in the contemporary education context in the U.S., these techniques are being used oppressively. With the exception of the Chicago Teacher's Strike in 2012 and the recent refusal of Seattle teachers to participate in testing, very little explicit resistance has surfaced to these oppressions. Research is needed to see what resistances are being constructed locally and globally and what impacts these resistances are having on teaching and learning.

As we have seen so far in the discussion, at its base contemporary schooling assumes inequality of intelligence, rather than equality, and takes advantage of oppressive techniques of power to maintain itself. What happens when we begin with assumptions of equality of intelligence and what follows from that assump-tion? If, instead, we see all intelligence as equal and we operate on principles of equipotentiality, learning becomes the focus and all positions are that of a learner of some kind. In this way, the child can know and be expert—everyone can. Here everyone counts.

Possibilities for Authentic Assessment

How else can we know that learning has occurred?

> When we engage in assessments, we make judgments as a result of assessments, we use judgment to design assessments, and, in turn, the design of assessments may affect the subsequent judgments we make. These three elements—values, judgment, and design—operate dynamically in any one assessment act.
>
> *(Murphy, 2012, p. 562).*

Research has shown other ways in which to value learning and to know that learning has occurred. Rogoff, Goodman-Turkanis, and Bartlett (2001) conceived of assessment as evaluating children's progress rather than achievement in some finite sense. In their work, teachers and students participated in collaborative activity in which teachers observed what children did, when and how they needed help formulating ideas and putting them in writing, using multiple resources, and to get a sense of student engagement in activities presented. Similarly, I have shown through my research with veteran classroom teachers Maryrita Maier and Lynn Gatto that assessment is an ongoing, integrated practice that helps them understand what their students are doing and what assistance they might need to accomplish their own learning goals (Larson & Maier, 2000; Larson & Marsh, 2005). Both teachers analyze their students' work on an ongoing basis to know where students are and what help, if any, they need to move forward in reaching their goals. By participating with their students in learning activities, both of these teachers were able to assess individual growth over time, understand how students' participation was transformed, and observed changes in responsibility for learning in ways that moved beyond standardization. Because they participated in learning activities with students, they knew what was learned and how it was learned. Their assessments shaped future activities rather than closing them down.

We need multiple, contextualized assessments that occur on an ongoing basis in order to begin to describe the complexity of human learning. Teachers need to be acknowledged as being the closest to the learner (outside of the learner her/himself). Teachers and students should develop and administer assessments together according to local curriculum goals. Local curriculum planning teams would need to have ongoing dialogue about what counts as knowing and what counts as warrant for knowing. They would need to be willing to have difficult conversations about values (Murphy, 2012). In this way, assessments could be more open and flexible, more appropriately connected to learning, and more educationally useful (Mislevy, 1997). These descriptions of authentic assessment are not new, nor will they be new to progressive teachers or teacher educators. I argue, however, that under current accountability mandates, they are less and less common, if not impossible.

Shifting to a poststructural perspective of knowledge production would afford teachers the opportunity to more fully understand, authentically use, and participate in the cultural practices children bring with them to the classroom. Using multiple data points in assessment of students' learning (e.g., teacher observations and reflections, learner self-assessment, locally constructed tests, conferences, written goal setting, and reflection) we can move beyond reductionist notions of achievement rooted in efficiency models of curriculum, toward authentic, practice-oriented understanding of what children and youth know and can produse. However, assessment still focuses on what the "student" subject position knows. Meaningful assessment needs to account for all learners, which in this case would include teachers, administrators, community members, and parents.

Do We Need a Test?

Some may argue that we still need a way for society to recognize that a student has completed a cycle of education. Using the same markers we have now (high school diploma, B.A., M.A., M.D., Ph.D.) could still work as long as assessment values are in line with starting with equality of intelligence and pedagogy as showing intelligence to itself. How will we know intelligence has seen itself? Rancière's version has the "master" listening while the learner recites what he/she has learned. However, this harkens back to transmission models of knowledge production and still holds the "master" in some kind of different space, and not an equitable one. Furthermore, it assumes the "master" knows what the intelligence is supposed to recite. This seems like a contradiction to me. We will know that intelligence has seen itself because we jointly participated in activities, saw problems resolved, and/or the curricular scenario would have changed.

"We the people" may still want a more generalizable way to know what children and youth have learned so that comparisons, both national and international, can be made. Darling-Hammond (2010) argues that the Programme for International Student Assessment (PISA, http://nces.ed.gov/surveys/pisa/) is a more authentic standardized assessment in that it asks students to apply their higher order thinking skills to real life issues/problems. PISA looks at fewer concepts but goes deeper into those concepts and accounts for both horizontal and vertical learning, whereas typical standardized tests focus only on vertical learning (Gutiérrez, 2008). In other words, this test allows for learners to take time with a problem (to think horizontally) rather than go directly to a predetermined correct answer (to think vertically).

Since it seems unlikely that international comparisons will go away, and we need a common way to know where we stand, maybe the PISA could be a part of an ongoing discussion where learning is seen as fundamentally fluid and constantly changing. However, what are the affordances and losses associated with using a standardized measure? Is it simply a matter of taking the "high stakes" off "test"? I think it is the standardization that is the key problem, but it is true that the stakes associated with testing in the U.S. are what is doing the most damage to students and teachers. If there were nothing at stake for an individual with the PISA (e.g., it was not a graduation requirement), what are the affordances and losses? Affordances include international comparison, state-to-state comparison, and a general sense of where we are in terms of our young knowing what we want them to know. However, I am concerned that the standardization of "what we want them to know" will become rigid over time, resulting in static knowledge that does not account for the fluidity of knowledge production. Losses include the value of knowing individual growth and development; however, maybe this is okay because we would have locally produced, situated assessments. I worry, however, about a slide back to teaching to the test so we compare favorably. Again, rigidity over fluidity becomes a concern as competitive achievement discourses could resurface and take hold. The ongoing assessments developed at the local level should account for this and could mediate the gap between skill/practice epistemologies.

Guiding Principles

In this chapter I have articulated what would change in curriculum, instruction, and assessment when we start from the assumption of equality of intelligence. I argued that we need to focus on curriculum that investigates what we need to know now in order to construct a plausible future. Following Rancière, instruction and pedagogy become about showing intelligence to itself. Assessment needs to be authentic, ongoing, and embedded in learning activities. I close the chapter with a set of guiding principles that may prove fruitful as we move to start over:

- *Curriculum, instruction, and assessment are fluid, constantly changing discursive productions in which metaphors of practices and networks supplant references to skills and packages.* Current conceptions of knowledge as a static body of information are outdated. Also outdated is the current curriculum practice of dissecting "knowledge" into skills that are then put into packages and sold as "the" way to teach a given content. Instead, we need to see knowledge as an ongoing social construction that needs to be understood through different and various means.
- *Curriculum teams that include teachers, administrators, parents, students, and community members would construct a district or school's curriculum using standards they*

determine to be relevant and meaningful to their community goals. All parties would share in the construction of purposes of curriculum and of the curriculum itself. In this way, the audience and purpose of curriculum are relevant and meaningful to the people it most affects in a given context.

- *We need both construction and deconstruction in order to stay relevant and fluid in the context of everyday life.* Given the fluidity of knowledge produsage in contemporary times, both processes are needed in a constant praxis (action and reflection) of curriculum production, implementation, and assessment.

- *Scenario planning can be used as a process to develop curriculum in the present that will prove sufficiently robust over several possible futures in ways that will critically engage learners.* Curriculum teams would use scenario planning in the process of curriculum development in ways that ensure local relevance and global impact. By planning for a plausible future, curriculum development moves away from static skills to authentic practices needed for sustainable futures.

- *Learning occurs through participation in social, cultural, and historical contexts that are mediated by interaction.* Learning happens through joint participation in curriculum development and implementation in which everyone is positioned as a learner and in which power/knowledge are mutually constituted. In this way, we move away from conceiving of learning as depositing information into empty heads.

- *Pedagogy becomes the process of showing intelligence to itself.* Through processes of emancipation, people come to see their own intelligence and the intelligence of others. Traditional conceptions of instruction as delivery are replaced. We will know that intelligence has seen itself because we jointly participated in activities, saw problems resolved, and/or the curricular scenario changed.

- *There is more than one answer to problems presented and all answers count.* No one knows the "correct" answer because we have moved beyond correctness measures of knowledge production. We can still account for expertise in content area knowledge of teachers (it does not mean there is equality of content knowledge even though there is equality of intelligence) through equipotential participation. In other words there is still a role for expertise even when there is no "correct" answer.

- *Build new knowledge rather than have old knowledge instructed and tested.* With scenario planning as a framework for developing a problem-posing curriculum, new knowledge can be prodused in innovative and creative ways. We would move away from traditional unidirectional concepts of knowledge as simply transmitted information that can be tested.

- *Power circulates in heterarchical social relations.* Following Foucault (1978), power is not a zero-sum commodity. Rather, power is capillary and is something everyone has. In equipotential participation, all power is available in the ongoing knowledge produsage process and circulated horizontally and vertically (heterarchically).

- *We need multiple, contextualized assessments that occur on an ongoing basis in order to begin to describe the complexity of human learning.* Mislevy (1997, p. 190) proposes an approach that takes authentic learning into account:

  > The essential elements of the approach are (1) understanding the important concepts and relationships in the learning area in order to know the aspects of students we need to talk about in the universe of discourse our assessment will generate and (2) determining what one needs to observe and how it depends on students' understandings, so as to structure assessment settings and tasks that will provide evidence about the above-mentioned aspects of students' understandings.

What should be known as cultures grow and change? How will we ensure that what we already know is a part of what new knowledge is being constructed? How will we know that learning has happened? I have offered some alternative answers to these questions in this chapter, alternatives to the transmission models of curriculum, to the static, standardized delivery model of instruction, and to the high-stakes assessment context in which we find ourselves. This rigid context not only has not resulted in a just and equitable system, it has exacerbated existing inequities to the point of tangible harm. I hope having some plausible alternative practices will lead to transformation, because the stakes are high indeed—too high.

Notes

1 Cf. Shannon, Patrick (2013). *Closer Readings of the Common Core.* Portsmouth, NH: Heinemann, for in-depth analyses of the Common Core.
2 I find Gee's (2011) definition of D/discourse helpful in this regard. "D"iscourse represents those ways of knowing and being associated with producing identities. "d"iscourse represents language in use.
3 The zone of proximal development is a collaborative, socially constructed activity in which a child's range of abilities is mutually constituted. It is a continuum of socially organized activity that shifts over time as the child becomes increasingly capable of supported independence (Gutiérrez, 2008).

5

IMAGINE WE CLIMB
THE MOUNTAIN

> There is no utopia to be sought, but simply a variety of struggles along a number of fronts, each one presupposing the equality of everyone.
>
> (May, 2010, p. 104)

Change is hard work. Sometimes when looking at the work that must be done it feels like an enormous mountain that we could not possibly climb. The teachers who are trying to work in the ways described in this book become frustrated and exhausted. But, then, nothing gets changed or the little that is changed feels too small to make an authentic difference in the system. Yet, we must begin the climb somewhere. This book is my attempt at a beginning and is one way I try to honor the hard work already going on.

While I do not want this to be a "how to" book, I do want to outline a plausible plan of action that uses the framework outlined in Chapter 2, the purpose of schooling in Chapter 3, and the principles of curriculum, instruction, and assessment in Chapter 4. Darling-Hammond (2010) outlines the policy needs for a rethinking of education that I draw on for this chapter. However, her focus remains on traditional notions of achievement as test score, which I believe is a key factor in why schools are not doing what they need to do for our children and youth. The plan of action I propose moves away from a narrow achievement focus.

Imagining the New

I imagine new spaces for learning that transform traditional content areas like English in ways that integrate contents in the service of knowledge produsage with locally constructed audiences and purposes. Local would be reconceived to include more global audiences since participation in knowledge produsage can be global, even when the "problem" might be local in a geographic sense. By understanding space as socially produced and producing, traditional spatial boundaries are blurred, especially in light of the mass participation engendered by new technologies. The institution of school must align itself with the concept of the equality of intelligence now that everyone can participate in meaningful learning on their own terms everywhere but in school. As May (2010, p. 104) suggests:

> What must characterize these institutions is an ongoing commitment to equality, one that shows not only in the formal roles that are adopted by the institution but in its unfolding activities. In that sense, any institutionalization of equality must display itself verbally, not just nominally.

With this lens, we could also remove the artificial spatial boundedness of school and conceive of learning as occurring in authentic spaces that do not need particularly marked physical spaces (community based spaces, webinars, social networking technologies). In this way, unproductive in/out of school binaries become irrelevant. Schools could become important public spaces where networked publics (boyd, 2008) come together to discuss problems and design solutions that enable sustainable futures (Facer, 2011). School would be a genuine public responsibility in which communities engage in a "collaborative workshop full of potential" (Fielding & Moss, 2011, p. 53) to plan projects of common interest rather than allow this planning to be directed by outside interests (e.g., corporations or textbook companies).

We would shift to building affinity spaces (Gee, 2004), both physical and virtual, where people gather around shared interests and like-minded issues rather than separating along race, class, gender, sexual orientation, linguistic, and ability lines, as is currently the case. I propose that we develop schools as spaces in which communities can build knowledge for their own purposes free of disciplinary power. These spaces can be free of oppression and exclusion, or what Foucault (1967) refers to as heterotopias.

Heterotopia is a concept used by Foucault (1967) to describe places and spaces that function in non-hegemonic conditions. These are spaces that are neither here nor there, that are simultaneously physical and mental, such as the space of a museum or the moment when you see yourself in the mirror. Foucault describes the ambivalence and interdependency of the heterotopia through the metaphor of the mirror: "In the mirror, I see myself there where I am not. . . . such is the utopia of the mirror. But it is also a heterotopia . . . absolutely real . . . and absolutely unreal" (1967, p. 3).

Foucault's call for a society with many heterotopias could refer to schools if they are transformed in ways I have discussed in this book. The Freedom Market project example illustrates how such spaces are constructed and used by community members to transform their neighborhood. Schools could not only be spaces that build on difference, but could also be spaces for escape from oppression, instead of spaces where oppression is strongest (Simmons, Lewis, & Larson, 2011). The Lunch Is Gross example demonstrates how school can breach spatial boundaries to fight against oppressive practices. Schools could be heterotopias of time and space where multiple spaces and historical times are juxtaposed. They would be a microcosm of the glocal (not in preparation for, but as an actual glocal space). Schools would not be heterotopias of deviation, or places where we place people who behave outside the norm, in that all students would be included in all spaces—no exceptions. School would become a space where the focus is on problem posing and problem solving with glocal audiences and purposes. In this way, schools could become more authentic contexts for societal changes, as resources for community transformation such as in Bigum's (n.d.) concept of knowledge producing schools. We could move from knowledge consumption to knowledge produsage in exciting ways.

Knowledge Producing Schools

The concept of knowledge producing schools has been written about by Bigum (2002) and by Rowan and Bigum (2010). In this work, they describe schools as spaces to construct diverse possible futures that are aware of what has changed (communication and participation structures) and what has not changed (the situation for poor children and children and youth from non-dominant groups) (Rowan & Bigum, 2010). Knowledge producing schools would respond to the need to change while not reproducing inequities. These schools account for the changed and changing relationship between schools and knowledge in a knowledge economy in ways that acknowledge the shift to knowledge production as they become community hubs of information and knowledge resources (Bigum, n.d.). I build on this concept here but shift from children and youth as producers to children, youth, teachers, administrators, parents, and community members as produsers of knowledge. Learners would produse knowledge from an early age and apply that knowledge in new ways to new, real world tasks with real world audiences. As Bigum (n.d.) argues:

> With support from groups in the community with specialist knowledge, schools could become a key location for the production, accumulation and dissemination of information about the local community, a hub for community informatics. Many teachers already do all kinds of interesting and potentially useful data collection with their students but in a 'fridge door' design sensibility the data is rarely kept, the analyses are not shared beyond the classroom (except on a family's fridge door) and it is unusual for the data to be stored and added to over time. With not much more effort and judicious use of CCTs, this could be changed. But importantly,

simply doing research, collecting data and doing analyses will matter little if the local community does not value the work. And this is the hard part. Schools would have to be at least partially remade in the minds of the local community. It would not require a wholesale change, but project-by-project it would be possible to build up a repertoire of research skills and products in consultation with local needs and interests. Here there is a clear opportunity to develop links with community groups with informatics projects and contribute to the transformation of regions.

In this way, community and school jointly produce new knowledge that can be used to solve real world problems with useful outcomes. The Lunch Is Gross example described in Chapter 2 offers a glimpse into what this might look like at the classroom level. Gatto and her students were a valuable resource of information for the community as they enacted social action that resulted in changing the school district's food vendor. They drew on community resources (a local news station and a local research firm) in the production of the documentary. As one result, food practices in the district were changed. Furthermore, the community became more aware of the problem of school lunches when they saw the film. The school became a resource for information instead of a storehouse, or a black box, into which we place our children. The Freedom Market takes this knowledge-producing-hub role to the community level as they work to provide healthy food and economic stability to a struggling neighborhood. The store is a key resource for information and knowledge about food and health as well as being a place to purchase healthier food. Facer's (2011) future school brings these roles together to produse knowledge for both the school and the community as they work for future learning. As Facer (2011, p. 10) suggests, we can

> reclaim the right of schools to act as resources for their communities to imagine and build the futures that they want rather than simply training them for the futures they have been given. To do so, we need to remember that the future is not set in stone, that technology is not some magical force driving us down one inevitable path and that education is also a force to be reckoned with when it comes to shaping progressive futures.

I have been working on a model that uses the principles articulated in this book to imagine an immersive virtual space of equipotential participation where local problems and possible solutions are played out first virtually then translated into real actions. The project would involve the use of new immersive computing technologies in schools to study how socio-technical innovations can transform the way students and neighborhood residents learn about and envision community transformation. Working with an inventor from a local technology university, we are planning to construct a three-dimensional, immersive learning environment to be housed at NEAD's Freedom School that first models assets, concerns, and opportunities imminent in the local neighborhood and then allows participants to re-envision the community according to community norms, values, and practices. Our specific goals are: (1) to improve the community's capacity to articulate their imagined futures, by (2) developing and assessing socio-technological tools that can visualize these changes, and (3) studying the reciprocal interactions and collaborative learning activities of students and community members in this unique situation.

By focusing on the nature of interaction in this space and how it is transformed, research could come to see how knowledge is prodused when "everybody comes" to focus on identifying a problem and finding a solution. The process would be the point, although it cannot just stay in the virtual. We would need to have an authentic purpose, like the community transformation possible if we focus on specific geographies such as those areas around the Freedom Market. Youth I have worked with have suggested a network of safe houses that could be an idea to play out first in the virtual space. We could use the virtual space to map the locations of the houses, network them, and then see the potential social and spatial changes that would result. Similar to knowledge producing schools, by bringing together in this space youth, architects, educators, politicians, and community service agencies among others, we could study the interaction and see the potential of these theories to make sense of knowledge produsage and the implications for constructing authentic spaces for learning. We could do this inclusively and with meaning. Meaning making and knowledge production would be the key in this model.

What Makes the Argument Plausible?

Part of what makes the argument I make in this book plausible is that children and youth and some adults are already working in these ways outside of school so it will not be unfamiliar to them. Do we want to be a part of this conversation? This question is a twist of Shirky's (2010) story about the 2005 subway bombings in London that describes what happened to news distribution after the bombings. People used Twitter and texting to get the word out about what happened all while the traditional news agency was waiting to release information to avoid panic. Shirky asks us whether we want to be a part of the conversation the people are already having or risk irrelevance. Shall schools continue on the path of irrelevance? I argue here that public schools can and should still play an important role in dismantling systems of inequality and, thus, that we should move past irrelevance and make the changes needed to start over with equality of intelligence as the founding principle. What are some things we need to do to start over?

hat We Need to Do Now

In order to start over, we need to consider doing the following:

1. *We need to change from assumptions of inequality to assumptions of equality.* We must begin from the place where all intelligence is equal and where teaching and learning become about showing intelligence to itself. People would have to experience emancipation themselves interdependently and intersubjectively, to see their own intelligence in order to understand how to show intelligence to itself. Following Rancière, we cannot instruct our way to emancipation and the understanding that all intelligence is equal; we have to find ways to show intelligence to itself. Perhaps the process of schools becoming community hubs where usable community knowledge is prodused would help this change in understanding as people participated in the process of emancipation themselves.

2. *We need to adopt a new purpose of schooling.* I argue that the new purpose of schooling should be *to facilitate human learning, meaning making, and knowledge production toward a just and equitable education system.* This new purpose would not necessarily invalidate other purposes (work/citizen, cognitive, social, etc.) but would place emphasis on meaning making and knowledge produsage for equity and justice. We would have to vigilantly watch that traditional purposes do not overtake the meaning making or the justice goals.

3. *Remove high-stakes testing; just stop them.* We should replace them with ongoing authentic assessments of learning and development. Several other countries already do this (Darling-Hammond, 2010). Assessments would be developed locally as long as there are no high stakes attached. We could still have traditional markers of completion (high school diploma, B.A., M.A., M.D., Ph.D.) where criteria for meeting those markers would be locally defined. We could use PISA if we need international comparison, although we would have to watch carefully that competitive achievement discourses do not resurface and take over.

4. *Value teachers and teacher education.* We need to move beyond seeing teachers and teacher education as the way to maintain the status quo and we need to elevate teacher work to a higher place in society. As the implementation of the Common Core Learning Standards illustrates, teachers in the U.S. are not valued as professionals with expertise in curriculum and pedagogy. This view is historically grounded in the view of teaching as "women's work" that is of lesser value (Britzman, 2003). Du Bois (1903/2002, p. 67) argued that teachers are educational leaders who

> should be prepared by long and rigorous courses of study similar to those which the world over have been designed to strengthen the intellectual powers, fortify character, and facilitate the transmission from age to age of the stores of the world's knowledges.

While he still operates from a transmission model of education, the points about the need for long and rigorous preparation of teachers remain important in contemporary times. We should continue to require in-depth teacher preparation (no 'alternative' quick fix ways into teaching—just because you went to school does not mean you can teach) and provide adequate financial support to do so. We have excellent undergraduate and graduate teacher preparation programs that we should focus on developing. We could follow Britzman's (2003, p. 49) dialogic reconstruction of teacher education that would recognize "that multiple realities, voices, and discourses conjoin and clash in the process of coming to know." Teacher education needs to offer safe spaces for changed and changing subjectivities as young teachers come to terms with who they are in relation to their students and to the profession. We need to remove artificial content boundaries and fractured spaces for identity development (Britzman, 2003) in order to focus on the integration of what we know for the purposes of knowledge produsage in the interest of local communities. Separating content areas is an artifact of the creation of fields of knowledge (Goodson, 1982), not of the nature of knowledge or knowing.

5. *Create local curriculum, instruction, and assessment planning teams* in which we would reconceive of schools as community hubs and as sources for knowledge produsage. In this model, schools would become local resources for knowledge and information as well as local sources for problem solving and community work. The Freedom Market project is one example of what this might look like at the community level. Gatto's film project is a school-based example. The curriculum teams would include school administration, teachers, paraprofessionals, community members (and several generations as Facer (2011) suggests), parents, and students. Including students is essential. Most reforms and discourses around education do not include students as part of the conversation. There are few spaces where children and youth have authentic voices in reform, let alone in curriculum planning. Some spaces do exist that value and incorporate youth voice, but they are typically not in schools. For example, Youth Speaks (2012), a national youth performance poetry project, and the Freechild Project (2012), youth participatory action research for social change, are both spaces where youth participation is primary. Rethinking Schools (2012) is a longstanding and highly respected teacher organized group that works to reform education for social justice and equity in ways that include student voice and is a valuable resource for changed practices.

6. *Fund schools adequately.* Research and the multitude of court cases around the country have shown that school funding is grossly inequitable in the U.S. education system and that those inequities fall along race and class lines (Karp, 2003). This is simply unacceptable. We have reverted to scenarios that are worse than before *Plessy v. Ferguson* (1896) that upheld the constitutionality

of separate but equal. Kozol's (2012a, 2012b, 2006) continued work has demonstrated that dilapidated and unsafe conditions exist across the country in under-resourced schools. Also unacceptable. As Darling-Hammond (2010, p. 309) argues, "we must finally address the deep and tenacious educational debt that holds our nation's future in hock, taking strong steps toward ensuring that every child has access to adequate school resources, facilities, and quality teachers." "We the people" can no longer sustain turning a blind eye to the inequitable education some of our children are receiving. Every child deserves a safe physical space and adequate resources for learning. All our children and youth count. My suggestion is to follow New Jersey's landmark *Abbott v. Burke* (2000) case in which the court ruled that minimum funding should be set at the level currently used in the richest, highest performing schools. However, we need to remove the concept of "performance" as a measure of worth (currently defined as a test score) from educational discourse and practice. Furthermore, the case ordered supplemental funding in the poorest districts to make up for past inequity. This seems like a no brainer. We simply cannot tolerate substandard education for any child in this country. Clearly money has not hurt rich kids and, thus, it matters a good deal, contrary to some educational economists' arguments that money does not matter (Hanushek, 1986).

What I have described in this book is not a utopian ideal, but a practical necessity. Children are being damaged and this is unacceptable. We can no longer stand by as deficit ideologies continue to support inequities. As Darling-Hammond (2010, p. 327) argues,

> If "no child left behind" is to be anything more than empty rhetoric, we will need a policy strategy that creates a 21st century curriculum for all students and supports it with thoughtful assessments, access to knowledgeable, well-supported teachers, and equal access to school resources.

By assuming all intelligence is equal and constructing spaces for learning that afford equipotential participation in produsage communities, we move closer to equitable and just schooling.

We cannot continue with schooling as it is today. We are too focused on achievement narrowly defined as tested skill. This is dangerous since it will lead (or has led) to a public unable to critically examine issues/texts (Shannon, 2011). And it is damaging children. What I have argued in this book is that we need to start over in schooling in the U.S. We must begin from an altogether different starting place, one that has different ontological and epistemological foundations—from a place of equality of intelligence and equipotential participation. We need to do this because we need a public that is able to work collaboratively, is focused on justice and equity, and can "read" the world and the word. We can do this. We must do this. Imagine.

REFERENCES

Abbott v. Burke (M-1336–98) (2000). http://lawlibrary.rutgers.edu/courts/supreme/
m-1336–98.opn.html Retrieved 1/6/2012.

Adler, M. J. (1982). *The Paidea proposal: An educational manifesto.* New York: Collier Macmillan.

Altwerger, B. & Strauss, S. (2002). The business behind testing. *Language Arts, 79(3),*
256–262.

Apple, M. (1990). *Ideology and curriculum.* New York: Routledge.

Arnove, R. & Torres, C. (1999). *Comparative education: The dialectic of the global and the local.*
Lanham, MD: Rowman & Littlefield.

Artiles, A. (2001). Toward an interdisciplinary understanding of equity and difference: The
case of the racialization of ability. *Educational Researcher, 40(9),* 431–445.

Au, W. (2007). High-stakes testing and curricular control: A qualitative metasynthesis.
Educational Researcher, 36(5), 258–267.

Bakhtin, M. (1981). *The dialogic imagination: Four essays by M. M. Bakhtin.* M. Holquist
(Ed.). Trans. C. Emerson & M. Holquist. Austin: University of Texas Press.

Barker, E. (Ed.). (1958). *The politics of Aristotle.* Trans. Ernest Barker. London: Oxford
University Press.

Baum-Snow, N. & Lutz, B. (2011). School desegregation, school choice, and changes in
residential location patterns by race. *American Economic Review, 101(7),* 3019–3046.

Bentham, J. (1791). *Panopticon.* London: T. Payne.

Berger, P. & Luckmann, T. (1967). *The social construction of reality: A treatise in the sociology
of knowledge.* New York: Anchor.

Biesta, G. (2011). The ignorant citizen: Mouffe, Rancière, and the subject of democratic
education. *Studies in Philosophy and Education, 30(2),* 141–153.

Biesta, G. (2009). Education and the democratic person: Towards a political conception
of democratic education. *Teachers College Record, 109(3),* 740–769.

Biggers, J. (2012). *Arizona unbound.* www.huffingtonpost.com/jeff-biggers/arizona
-unbound_b_1232285.html Retrieved 2/20/2012.

Bigum, C. (n.d.). *Rethinking schools and community: The knowledge producing school.* www.
deakin.edu.au/education/lit/kps/pubs/region.rtf Retrieved 6/7/2007.

Bigum, C. (2002). The knowledge producing school: Rethinking computing and communication technologies in schools. *Professional Voice, 2(2),* 1–3.

Blanchett, W. J. (2006). Disproportionate representation of African American students in special education: Acknowledging the role of white privilege and racism. *Educational Researcher, 35(6),* 24–28.

Bloom, B. (1969). *Taxonomy of educational objectives.* New York: D. McKay Co.

Bobbitt, F. (1918). *The curriculum.* Cambridge, MA: Riverside Press.

Bode, B. (1927). *Modern educational theories.* New York: Macmillan.

Bourdieu, P. & Passeron, J. C. (1990). *Reproduction in education, society and culture* (Vol. 4). London/Thousand Oaks, CA: Sage.

Bowles, S. & Gintis, H. (1980). *Schooling in capitalist America: Educational reform and the contradictions of economic life.* New York: Basic Books.

boyd, d. (2008). Why youth social network sites: The role of networked publics in teenage social life. In D. Buckingham (Ed.), *Youth, identity, and digital media,* pp. 119–142. Cambridge, MA: MIT Press.

Brameld, T. (1956). *Toward a reconstructed philosophy of education.* New York: Dryden.

Britzman, D. (2003). *Practice makes practice: A critical study of learning to teach.* Albany, NY: SUNY Press.

Bruner, J. (1960). *The process of education.* Cambridge, MA: Harvard University Press.

Bruns, A. (2008). *Blogs, Second Life, and beyond: From production to produsage.* New York: Lang.

Burrello, L. C., Sailor, W., & Kleinhammer-Tramill, J. (Eds.). (2013). *Unifying educational systems: Leadership and policy perspectives.* New York: Routledge.

Charters, W. (1909). *Methods of teaching developed from a functional standpoint.* Chicago: Row, Peterson & Company.

Cherryholmes, C. (1988). *Power and criticism: Poststructural investigations in education.* New York: Teachers College Press.

Christensen, L., Hansen, M., Peterson, B., Schlessman, E., & Watson, D. (2012). *Rethinking elementary education.* Milwaukee, WI: Rethinking Schools.

Cole, M. (1996). *Cultural psychology: A once and future discipline.* Cambridge, MA: Belknap Press of Harvard University Press.

Coles, G. (2003). *Reading the naked truth: Literacy, legislation and lies.* Portsmouth, NH: Heinemann.

Collins, A. & Halverson, R. (2009). *Rethinking education in the age of technology: The digital revolution and schooling in America.* New York: Teachers College Press.

Common Core Standards (2012a). www.corestandards.org Retrieved 2/12/2012.

Common Core Standards for English Language Arts and Literacy in History/Social Studies, Science and Technical Subjects (2012b). www.corestandards.org/assets/CCSSI_ELA%20Standards.pdf Retrieved 7/26/2012.

Counts, G. S. (1932). *Dare the schools build a new social order.* New York: World Book.

Cuban, L. (1994). *How teachers taught: Constancy and change in American classrooms 1890–1980.* New York: Longman.

Darling-Hammond, L. (2010). *The flat world and education: How America's commitment to equity will determine our future.* New York: Teachers College Press.

de Alba, A., González-Gaudiano, E., Lankshear, C., & Peters, M. (2000). *Curriculum in the postmodern condition.* New York: Lang.

de Certeau, M. (1984). *The practice of everyday life.* Berkeley: University of California Press.

deMarrais, K. B. & LeCompte, M. D. (1995). *The way schools work: A sociological analysis of education* (2nd ed.). White Plains, NY: Longman.

Democrat and Chronicle (2013). www.democratandchronicle.com/article/20130617/ NEWS01/306170040/graduation-rate-rochester-monroe-county-schools Retrieved 6/17/2013.

Derrida, J. (1967/1976). *Of grammatology.* Trans. G. Spivak. Baltimore, MD: Johns Hopkins University Press.

Dewey, J. (1938). *Experience and education.* New York: Macmillan.

Dewey, J. (1899). *The school and society.* Chicago: University of Chicago Press.

Dixon-Román, E. (2010). Inheritance and an economy of difference: The importance of supplementary education. In L. Lin, E. W. Gordon, & H. Varenne (Eds.), *Educating comprehensively: Varieties of educational experiences,* pp. 95–112. Lewiston, NY: Edwin Mellen Press.

Doyle, W. (1992). Curriculum and pedagogy. In P. Jackson (Ed.), *Handbook of research on teaching,* pp. 486–516. New York: Macmillan.

Du Bois, W. E. B. (1903/2002). The training of Negroes for social power. In E. Provenzo, Jr. (Ed.), *Du Bois on education,* pp. 65–73. Walnut Creek, CA: Altamira.

Duncan, A. (2013, April). Choosing the right battles: Remarks and a conversation. Special invited address at the American Educational Research Association, San Francisco, CA.

Duncan, G. & Murnane, R. (2011). *Whither opportunity? Rising inequality, schools and children's life chances.* New York: Russell Sage Foundation.

Egan, K. (2008). *The future of education: Reimagining our schools from the ground up.* New Haven, CT: Yale University Press.

Ellsworth, E. (1989). Why doesn't this feel empowering? Working through the repressive myths of critical pedagogy. *Harvard Educational Review, 59(3),* 297–324.

Erevelles, N. (2000). Educating unruly bodies: Critical pedagogy, disability studies, and the politics of schooling. *Educational theory, 50(1),* 25–47.

Facer, K. (2011). *Learning futures: Education, technology, and social change.* New York: Routledge.

Ferri, B. & Connor, D. (2005). Tools of exclusion: Race, disability, and (re) segregated education. *Teachers College Record, 107(3),* 453–474.

Fielding, M. & Moss, P. (2011). *Radical education and the common school: A democratic alternative.* New York: Routledge.

Fine, M. (1991). *Framing dropouts: Notes on the politics of an urban public high school.* Albany, NY: State University of New York Press.

Foucault, M. (1991). Governmentality. In G. Burchell, C. Gordon, & P. Miller (Eds.), *The Foucault effect: Studies in governmentality,* pp. 87–104. Hemel Hempstead, UK: Harvester Wheatsheaf.

Foucault, M. (1979). *Discipline and punish: The birth of the prison.* Trans. A. Sheridan. New York: Random House.

Foucault, M. (1978). *The history of sexuality: Vol. 1. An introduction.* Trans. R. Hurley. New York: Vintage.

Foucault, M. (1967). *Of other spaces.* http://foucault.info/documents/heteroTopia/foucault. heteroTopia Retrieved 3/9/09.

Free Child Project (2012). www.freechild.org/PAR.htm Retrieved 1/6/2012.

Freire, P. (1970). *Pedagogy of the oppressed.* New York: Continuum.

Freire, P. & Macedo, D. (1987). *Literacy: Reading the word and the world.* South Hadley, MA: Bergin & Garvey.

Gates Foundation (2012). www.gatesfoundation.org/highschools/Documents/fewer-clearer-higher-standards.pdf Retrieved 12/28/2012.

Gatto, L. (2013). "Lunch is gross": Gaining access to powerful literacies. *Language Arts, 90(4)*, 241–252.

Gatto, L. (2012a). Negotiating authority through whole class talk. Ph.D. dissertation, University of Rochester.

Gatto, L. (2012b). www.teachertube.com/viewVideo.php?video_id=11129&title= LUNCH_IS_GROSS Retrieved 7/20/2012.

Gay, G. (2010). *Culturally responsive teaching: Theory, research, and practice.* New York: Teachers College Press.

Gee, J. P. (2013a, April). New media literacies and learning: The role of social media in reducing poverty. Paper presented at the annual meeting of the American Educational Research Association, San Francisco, CA.

Gee, J. P. (2013b). *The anti-education era: Creating smarter students through digital learning.* New York: Palgrave

Gee, J. P. (2011). *An introduction to discourse analysis: Theory and method.* New York: Routledge.

Gee, J. P. (2010). *New digital media and learning as an emerging area and "worked examples" as one way forward.* Cambridge, MA: MIT Press.

Gee, J. P. (2007). *What video games have to teach us about learning and literacy. Second Edition.* New York: Palgrave Macmillan.

Gee, J. P. (2004). *Situated language and learning: A critique of traditional schooling.* New York: Routledge.

Giroux, H. (1983). Theories of reproduction and resistance in the new sociology of education: A critical analysis. *Harvard Educational Review, 53(3)*, 261–293.

Godin, S. (2008). *Tribes: We need you to lead us.* New York: Portfolio Trade.

Goodlad, J. (1984). *A place called school: Prospects for the future.* New York: McGraw-Hill.

Goodman, K. S. (1987). *Language and thinking in school: A whole-language curriculum.* New York: Richard C. Owen.

Goodson, I. (1982). *School subjects and curriculum change: Case studies in curriculum history.* London: Croom Helm.

Gore, J. (1998). Disciplining bodies: On the continuity of power relations in pedagogy. In T. Popkewitz & M. Brennan (Eds.), *Foucault's challenge: Discourse, knowledge, and power in education,* pp. 231–251. New York: Teachers College Press.

Guisbond, L., Neill, M., & Schaeffer, B. (2012). *NCLB's lost decade for educational progress: What can we learn from this policy failure.* MA: Fair Test. http://fairtest.org/NCLB-lost -decade-report-home

Gutiérrez, K. (2008). Developing a sociocritical literacy in the third space. *Reading Research Quarterly, 43(2)*, 148–164.

Gutiérrez, K. (2007). "Sameness as fairness": The new tonic of equality and opportunity. In J. Larson (Ed.), *Literacy as snake oil: Beyond the quick fix,* pp. 109–122. New York: Lang.

Gutiérrez, K. & Larson, J. (2007). Discussing expanded spaces for learning. *Language Arts, 85(1)*, 69–77.

Gutiérrez, K. & Rogoff, B. (2003). Cultural ways of learning: Individual traits or reper-toires of practice. *Educational Researcher, 32(5)*, 19–25.

Gutiérrez, K. D. (1995). Unpackaging academic discourse. *Discourse processes, 19(1)*, 21–37.

Gutiérrez, R. (2012). Context matters: How should we conceptualize equity in mathematics education. In B. Herbel-Eisenmann, J. Choppin, D. Wagner, & D. Pimm (Eds.), *Equity in discourse for mathematics education: Theories, practices and policies,* pp. 17–33. New York: Springer.

Gutmann, A. (1987/1999). *Democratic education.* Princeton, NJ: Princeton University Press.

Hanushek, E. (1986). The economics of schooling: Production and efficiency in public schools. *Journal of Economic Literature, 24(3),* 1141–1177.

Hayman, R. (1998). *The smart culture: Society, intelligence, and law.* New York: New York University Press.

Heath, S. B. (1983). What no bedtime story means: Narrative skills at home and school. *Language in Society, 11(1),* 49–76.

Herbart, J. (1904). *Outline of educational doctrine.* Trans. Alex Flange. New York: Macmillan.

Hirsch, E. D. (1987). *Cultural literacy: What every American needs to know.* Boston: Houghton Mifflin.

Hirst, P. (1974). *Knowledge and the curriculum.* London: Routledge and Kegan Paul.

hooks, b. (1994). *Teaching to transgress: Education as the practice of freedom.* New York: Routledge.

Hout, M. & Elliott, S. W. (Eds.). (2011). *Incentives and test-based accountability in education.* Washington, DC: National Academy Press.

Hunter, M. (1982). *Mastery teaching.* El Segundo, CA: TIP Press.

Hursh, D. (2008). *High-stakes testing and the decline of teaching and learning: The real crisis in education.* New York: Rowman & Littlefield.

Irvine, P. D. & Larson, J. (2007). Literacy packages in practice: Constructing academic disadvantage. In J. Larson (Ed.), *Literacy as snake oil: Beyond the quick fix. Second edition.* New York: Lang.

Isaacs, M., Huang, L., Hernandez, M., & Echo-Hawk (2005). *The road to evidence: The intersection of evidence-based practices and cultural competence in children's mental health.* http://scholar.googleusercontent.com/scholar?q=cache:Qox9nPUyB3gJ:scholar.google.com/+Isaacs,+Huang,+Hernandez,+Echo-Hawk,+2006&hl=en&as_sdt=0,33 Retrieved 3/13/2012.

Ito, M., Baumer, S., Bittanti, M., boyd, d., Cody, R., Herr, B., Horst, H. A., Lange P. G., Mahendran, D., Martinez, K., Pascoe, C. J., Perkel, D., Robinson, L., Sims, C., & Tripp, L. (with J. Antin, M. Finn, A. Law, A. Manion, S. Mitnick, D. Schlossberg, & S. Yardi) (2010). *Hanging out, messing around, and geeking out: Kids living and learning with new media.* Cambridge, MA: MIT Press.

Jackson, P. (1992). *Untaught lessons.* New York: Teachers College Press.

Janks, H. (2010). *Literacy and power.* New York: Routledge.

Jefferson, T. (1784/1954). *The Founders' Constitution, Volume 1, Chapter 18, Document 16.* Chicago: University of Chicago Press. http://press-pubs.uchicago.edu/founders/documents/v1ch18s16.html Retrieved 8/6/2012.

Jenkins, H. (2006). *Convergence culture: Where old and new media collide.* New York: New York University Press.

Jenkins, H., Ford, S., & Green, J. (2013). *Spreadable media: Creating value and meaning in a networked culture.* New York: New York University Press.

Karp, S. (2003). State by state battle for funding equity gets mixed results. *Rethinking schools online, 18(1).* www.rethinkingschools.org/archive/18_01/just181.shtml

Kincheloe, J. (1993). *Toward a critical politics of teacher thinking: Mapping the postmodern.* Westport, CT: Bergin & Garvey.

King, J. E. (1994). The purpose of schooling for African American children: Including cultural knowledge. In E. Hollins, J. King, & W. Hayman (Eds.), *Teaching diverse populations: Formulating a knowledge base,* pp. 25–56. New York: SUNY Press.

Kliebard, H. (2004). *The struggle for the American curriculum* (3rd ed.). New York: Routledge

Kohn, A. (1999). *The schools our children deserve: Moving beyond traditional classrooms and "tougher standards."* New York: Houghton Mifflin.

Kozol, J. (2012a). *Savage inequalities: Children in America's schools.* New York: Broadway Books.

Kozol, J. (2012b). *Fire in the ashes: Twenty-five years among the poorest children in America.* New York: Crown.

Kozol, J. (2006). *The shame of a nation.* New York: Crown.

Kress, G. (2010). *Multimodality: A social semiotic approach to contemporary communication.* New York: Routledge.

Ladson-Billings, G. (2011). Through a glass darkly: The persistence of race in education research and scholarship. *Educational Researcher, 41(4),* 115–120.

Ladson-Billings, G. (2006). From the achievement gap to the education debt: Understanding achievement in U.S. schools. *Educational Researcher, 35(10),* 3–12.

Ladson-Billings, G. (1995). Toward a theory of culturally relevant pedagogy. *American Educational Research Journal, 32(3),* 465–491.

Lambert, M., Boerst, T., & Graziani, F. (2011). Organizational resources in the service of school-wide ambitious teaching practice. *Teachers College Record, 113(7),* 1361–1400.

Lammers, J. C. (2013). Fan girls as teachers: Examining pedagogic discourse in an online fan site. *Learning, Media and Technology.* Advance online publication. DOI: 10.1080/17439884.2013.764895.

Lankshear, C. & Knobel, M. (2011). *Literacies: Social, cultural, and historical perspectives.* New York: Lang.

Lankshear, C. & Knobel, M. (2010). *DIY media.* New York: Lang.

Lankshear, C. & Knobel, M. (2006). *New literacies: Everyday practices and classroom learning.* New York: Open University Press.

Larson, J. (2013). Operationalizing the neo-liberal common good. In P. Shannon (Ed.), *Closer readings of the Common Core.* Portsmouth, NH: Heinemann.

Larson, J. (Ed.). (2007). *Literacy as snake oil: Beyond the quick fix. Second edition.* New York: Lang.

Larson, J., Hanny, C., Duckles, J., Moses, G., Wu, X., Moses, R., Nelson, K., Smith, W., & Smith, J. (2013, April). Community literacies as shared resources for transformation. Paper presented at the annual meeting of the American Educational Research Association, San Francisco, CA.

Larson, J., Hanny, C., Moses, G., & Boatwright, T. (2012, April). Spaces of geographic convergence culture. Paper presented at the annual meeting of the American Educational Research Association, Vancouver, British Columbia.

Larson, J. & Moses, G. (2012, April). Freedom Market: Taking back a corner market. Paper presented at the annual meeting of the American Educational Research Association, Vancouver, British Columbia.

Larson, J., Allen, A-R., & Osborn, D. (2010). Curriculum and the publishing industry. In B. McGraw, E. Baker, & P. Peterson (Eds.), *International Encyclopedia of Education, 3rd Edition,* pp. 368–373. Philadelphia, PA: Elsevier.

Larson, J. & Marsh, J. (2005). *Making literacy real: Theories and practices for learning and teaching.* Thousand Oaks, CA: Sage.

Larson, J. & Maier, M. (2000). Co-authoring classroom texts: "Shifting Participant Roles in Writing Activity." *Research in the Teaching of English, 34(4),* 468–497.

Lave, J. & Wenger, E. (1991). *Situated learning: Legitimate peripheral participation.* Cambridge: Cambridge University Press.

Leander, K. M. (2007). "You won't be needing your laptops today": Wired bodies in the wireless classroom. In M. Knobel & C. Lankshear (Eds.), *A new literacies sampler,* pp. 25–48. New York: Lang.

Lee, C. D. (2001). Is October Brown Chinese? A cultural modeling activity system for underachieving students. *American Educational Research Journal, 38(1),* 97–141.

Lefebvre, H. (1991). *The production of space.* Trans. D. Nicholson-Smith. Oxford/Cambridge, MA: Blackwell.

Leitsyyna, P. (2007). Corporate testing: Standards, profit, and the demise of the public sphere. *Teacher Education Quarterly, 34(2),* 59–94.

Leslie, M. (2013). *The vexing legacy of Lewis Terman.* http://alumni.stanford.edu/get/page/magazine/article/?article_id=40678 Retrieved 8/7/2013.

Lewis, C., Perry, R., & Murata, A. (2006). How should research contribute to instructional improvement? The case of lesson study. *Educational Researcher, 35(3),* 3–14.

Linn, R. (2000). Assessments and accountability. *Educational Researcher, 29(2),* 4–16.

Luke, C. & Gore, J. (Eds.). (1992). *Feminisms and critical pedagogy.* London and New York: Routledge.

Lyotard, J. F. (1979/1989). *The postmodern condition: Report on knowledge.* Minneapolis: University of Minnesota Press.

MacDonald, J. (1995). The autobiographical statement. In W. Pinar (Ed.), *Curriculum theorizing: The reconceptualists,* pp. 3–4. Berkeley, CA: McCutcheon.

Mann, H. (1848/1957). Twelfth annual report of the [Massachusetts] board of education. In L. Cremin (Ed.), *The republic and the school: Horace Mann and the education of free men.* New York: Teachers College Press.

Marx, K. (1867/1977). *Capital: A critique of political economy.* S. Moore & E. Aveling, trans. F. Engels, ed. New York: International.

May, T. (2010). *Contemporary political movements and the thought of Jacques Rancière: Equality in action.* Edinburgh: Edinburgh University Press.

McClintock, N. (2011). From industrial garden to food desert: Demarcated devaluation in the flatlands of Oakland, California. In A. H. Alkon & J. Agyeman (Eds.), *Cultivating food justice: Race, class, and sustainability,* pp. 89–120. Cambridge, MA: MIT Press.

McIntyre, A. (2008). *Participatory action research.* London: Sage.

McLaren, P. (1994). *Life in schools: An introduction to critical pedagogy in the foundations of education.* New York: Longman.

McNeil, J. (1990). *Curriculum: A comprehensive introduction.* New York: HarperCollins.

McNeil, L. (2000). *Contradictions of school reform: Educational costs of standardized testing.* New York: Routledge.

Mehan, H. (1979). *Learning lessons: Social organization in the classroom.* Cambridge, MA: Harvard University Press.

Mills, C. W. (2000). *The power elite.* Oxford: Oxford University Press.

Mislevy, R. (1997). Postmodern test theory. In A. Lesgold, M. Feuer, & A. Black (Eds.), *Transitions in work and learning: Implications for assessment,* pp. 180–199. National Academy of Sciences. www.nap.edu/catalog/5790.html Retrieved 4/29/2012.

Moll, L. (2000). Inspired by Vygotsky: Ethnographic experiments in education. In C. Lee & P. Smagorinsky (Eds.), *Vygotskian perspectives on literacy research: Constructing meaning through collaborative inquiry,* pp. 256–268. Cambridge: Cambridge University Press.

Moll, L. C., Amanti, C., Neff, D., & Gonzalez, N. (1992). Funds of knowledge for teaching: Using a qualitative approach to connect homes and classrooms. *Theory into practice, 31(2),* 132–141.

Morrell, E. (2008). *Critical literacy and urban youth: Pedagogies of access, dissent, and liberation.* New York: Routledge.

Murphy, S. (2012). Towards knowing well and doing well: Assessment and early childhood education. In J. Larson & J. Marsh (Eds.), *Handbook of early childhood literacy. Second edition.* London: Sage.

National Center for Educational Statistics (NCES). (2011a). *The nation's report card: Mathematics 2011.* Available online at http://nces.ed.gov/nationsreportcard/

National Center for Educational Statistics (NCES). (2011b). *The nation's report card: Reading 2011.* Available online at http://nces.ed.gov/nationsreportcard/

National Center for Educational Statistics (NCES). (2008). *Drop-out rates of high school students.* http://nces.ed.gov/ Retrieved 5/5/2009.

New York City Board of Education. (2011). http://schools.nyc.gov/Academics/default.htm Retrieved 12/4/2011.

Ngo, B. (2006). Learning from the margins: The education of Southeast and South Asian Americans in context. *Race, Ethnicity, and Education, 9(1),* 51–65.

Nichols, S. & Berliner, D. (2007). *Collateral damage: How high-stakes testing corrupts America's schools.* Cambridge, MA: Harvard Education Press.

Noguera, P. (2013). Education, racial inequality and the future of America. Distinguished lecture presented at the annual meeting of the American Educational Research Association, San Francisco.

Nussbaum, M. (2011). *Creating capabilities: The human development approach.* Cambridge: Belknap Press.

Orfield, G. (2001). *Schools more separate: Consequences of a decade of resegregation.* Civil Rights Project, Harvard University. www.law.harvard.edu/groups/civilrights/publications/resegregation01/schoolsseparate.pdf Retrieved 6/5/2012.

Osborn, D. (2007). Digging up the family tree: America's forced choice. In J. Larson (Ed.), *Literacy as snake oil: Beyond the quick fix. Second edition,* pp. 171–188. New York: Lang.

Partnership for 21st Century Skills (2007). *21st century skills standards: A partnership for 21st century skills.* Epaper. www.21stcenturyskills.org/documents/21st_century_skills_standards.pdf Retrieved 1/16/2009.

Peters, M. & Burbules, N. (2004). *Poststructuralism and educational research.* Oxford: Rowman & Littlefield.

Pinar, W. (1995). *Understanding curriculum.* New York: Lang.

Plessy v. Ferguson (1896). PBS. www.pbs.org/wnet/jimcrow/stories_events_plessy.html Retrieved 7/9/13.

Popham, W. (2004). Curriculum, instruction, and assessment: Amiable allies or phony friends? *Teachers College Record, 106(3),* 417–428.

Postman, N. (1995). *The end of education.* New York: Vintage Books.

Pothukuchi, K. (2005). Attracting supermarkets to inner-city neighborhoods: Economic development outside the box. *Economic Development Quarterly, 19(3),* 232–244.

Programme for International Student Achievement (2011). www.pisa.oecd.org/pages/0,3417,en_32252351_32235907_1_1_1_1_1,00.html Retrieved 12/21/2011.

Rancière, J. (1991). *The ignorant schoolmaster: Five lessons in intellectual emancipation.* Stanford, CA: Stanford University Press.

Rancière, J. & Corcoran, S. (2010). *Dissensus: On politics and aesthetics.* New York: Continuum.

Rethinking Schools. (2012). www.rethinkingschools.org/index.shtml Retrieved 1/6/2012.

Rheingold, H. (2002). *Smart mobs: The next social revolution.* Cambridge, MA: Basic Books.

Robinson, S. K. (2010a). *Out of our minds: Learning to be creative.* Edina, MN: Capstone.

Robinson, S. K. (2010b). *Bring on the learning revolution.* www.ted.com/talks/sir_ken_ robinson_bring_on_the_revolution.html Retrieved 6/20/2013.

Rochester City School District (2011). www.rcsdk12.org/197310416151348457/blank/ browse.asp?A=383&BMDRN=2000&BCOB=0&C=55396 Retrieved 12/4/2011.

Rogoff, B. (2011). *Developing destinies: A Mayan midwife and town.* Oxford: Oxford University Press.

Rogoff, B. (2008). Observing sociocultural activity on three planes: Participatory appropriation, guided participation, and apprenticeship. In K. Hall, P. Murphy, & J. Soler (Eds.), *Pedagogy and practice: Culture and identities,* pp. 58–74. London: Sage.

Rogoff, B. (2003). *The cultural nature of human development.* New York: Oxford University Press.

Rogoff, B. (1994). Developing understanding of the idea of communities of learners. *Mind, Culture, and Activity, 1(4),* 209–229.

Rogoff, B., Turkanis, C. G., & Bartlett, L. (2001). *Learning together: Children and adults in a school community.* New York: Oxford University Press.

Roid, G. (2011). *Stanford Binet Intelligence Scales (SB5). Fifth edition.* Rolling Meadows, IL: Riverside Publishing.

Rose, M. (2009). *Why school?* New York: The New Press.

Rowan, L. & Bigum, C. (2010). At the hub of it all: Knowledge producing schools as sites for educational and social innovation. In D. Clandfield & G. Martell (Eds.), *The school as community hub: Beyond education's iron cage,* pp. 185–203. Ottawa: Canadian Centre for Policy Alternatives.

Rowan, L. & Bigum, C. (1997). The future of technology and literacy teaching in primary learning situations and contexts. In C. Lankshear, C. Bigum, C. Currant, B. Green, E. Honan, J. Murray, W. Morgan, I. Snyder, & M. Wild (Eds.), *Digital rhetorics: Literacies and technologies in education—current and future directions.* Canberra, ACT: DEETYA.

Rugg, H. O. (1936). *American life and the school curriculum: Next steps toward schools of living.* New York: Ginn and Company.

Saltman, R. (2012). *The failure of corporate school reform.* St. Paul, MN: Paradigm.

Shannon, P. (2011). *Reading wide awake: Politics, pedagogies, and possibilities.* New York: Teachers College Press.

Shannon, P. (1989). *Broken promises: Reading instruction in twentieth-century America.* Westport, CT: Praeger.

Shepard, L. A. (1990). Inflated test score gains: Is the problem old norms or teaching the test? *Educational Measurement: Issues and Practice, 9(3),* 15–22.

Shirky, C. (2010). *Cognitive surplus: Creativity and generosity in a connected age.* New York: Penguin.

Shirky, C. (2008). *Here comes everybody: The power of organizing without organizations.* New York: Penguin.

Shulman, L. (1987). Knowledge and teaching: Foundations of the new reform. *Harvard Educational Review, 57(1),* 1–22.

Simmons, C., Lewis, C., & Larson, J. (2011). Narrating identities: Schools as touchstones of endemic marginalization. *Anthropology and Education Quarterly, 42(2),* 121–133.

Skinner, B. (1954). The science of learning and the art of teaching. *Harvard Educational Review, 24(2),* 86–97.

Smith, D. (2003). Curriculum and teaching face globalization. In W. Pinar (Ed.), *International handbook of curriculum research,* pp. 35–51. Mahwah, NJ: Lawrence Erlbaum Associates.

Soja, E. (2010). *Seeking spatial justice*. Minneapolis: University of Minnesota Press.

Soja, E. (2003). *Postmodern geographies*. London: Verso.

Spector, J. (2012). www.democratandchronicle.com/article/20120920/NEWS01/309200049/Census%20Rochester%20childhood%20poverty Retrieved 5/14/2013.

Spencer, H. (1860). *Education*. New York: Appleton.

Spring, J. (2012). *Education networks: Power, wealth, cyberspace, and the digital mind*. New York: Routledge.

Spring, J. (2011). *American education* (15th ed.). New York: McGraw-Hill.

Street, B. (1995). *Social literacies: Critical approaches to literacy in development, ethnography, and education*. New York: Addison-Wesley.

Taba, H. (1962). *Curriculum development: Theory and practice*. New York: Harcourt, Brace & World, Inc.

Tatum, B. (2007). *Can we talk about race: And other conversations in an era of school resegregation*. Boston: Beacon Press.

The Week (2013). http://theweek.com/article/index/218167/americarsquos-food-deserts Retrieved 6/16/13.

Thorndike, E. (1913). *Educational psychology vol. 2: The psychology of learning*. New York: Teachers College Press.

Tyack, D. & Cuban, L. (1995). *Tinkering toward utopia: A century of public school reform*. Cambridge, MA: Harvard University Press.

Tyler, R. (1949). *Basic principles of curriculum and instruction*. Chicago: University of Chicago Press.

U.S. Census. (2010). www.census.gov Retrieved 7/12/13.

U.S. Department of Agriculture (USDA). (2013). http://apps.ams.usda.gov/fooddeserts/foodDeserts.aspx Retrieved 6/16/13.

U.S. Department of Education. (2013). *For each and every child: A strategy for education equity and excellence*. Washington, DC: U.S. Department of Education.

U.S. Department of Education (USDOE). (2012a). http://www2.ed.gov/nclb/landing.jhtml?src=ln Retrieved 1/15/2012.

U.S. Department of Education (USDOE). (2012b). http://www2.ed.gov/programs/racetothetop/index.html Retrieved 1/15/2012.

U.S. Department of Education Office of Inspector General (USDO19). (2006). *The Reading First Program's grant application process final inspection report*. www.ed.gov/about/offices/list/oig/aireports/i13f0017.pdf Retrieved 1/15/2012.

Valencia, P. (2010). *Dismantling contemporary deficit thinking: Educational thought and practice*. New York: Routledge.

Vygotsky, L. (1986). *Thought and language*. Cambridge, MA: MIT press.

Vygotsky, L. (1978). *Mind in society*. Cambridge, MA: Harvard University Press.

Weiler, K. (1988). *Women teaching for change: Gender, class and power*. South Hadley, MA: Bergin & Garvey.

Wikipedia. (2011). http://en.wikipedia.org/wiki/Common_good Retrieved 9/18/2011.

William, D. (2000). The meanings and consequences of educational assessments. *Critical Quarterly, 42(1),* 105–127.

Youth Speaks (2012). http://youthspeaks.org/word/ Retrieved 1/6/2012.

INDEX

Note: Page numbers followed by 'f' refer to figures and followed by 't' refer to tables.

Printed by PGSTL